To Father Demske
— who is a whole
man. Doni Patees
3/74

FRANCIS BACON AND SOCIALIZED SCIENCE

Publication No. 906

AMERICAN LECTURE SERIES®

A Monograph in

The BANNERSTONE DIVISION of
AMERICAN LECTURES IN PHILOSOPHY

Edited by

MARVIN FARBER
State University of New York at Buffalo
Buffalo, New York

It is the purpose of this Series to give representation to all important tendencies and all points of view in Philosophy, without any implied concurrence on the part of the Editor and Publisher.

Francis Bacon and Socialized Science.

By

ANTOINETTE MANN PATERSON
Professor, Department of Philosophy
State University of New York College at Buffalo
Buffalo, New York

CHARLES C THOMAS • PUBLISHER
Springfield • Illinois • U.S.A.

Published and Distributed Throughout the World by

CHARLES C THOMAS • PUBLISHER
Bannerstone House
301-327 East Lawrence Avenue, Springfield, Illinois, U.S.A.

© *1973, by* CHARLES C THOMAS • PUBLISHER
ISBN 0-398-02867-2
Library of Congress Catalog Card Number 73-5588

Library of Congress Cataloging in Publication Data
Paterson, Antoinette Mann.
Francis Bacon and socialized science.

(American lecture series, publication no. 906. A monograph in the Bannerstone
division of American lectures in philosophy)

Bibliography: p.
1. Bacon, Francis, Viscount St. Albans, 1561-1626.
I. Title.
B1198.P36   192 [B]   73-5588
ISBN 0-398-02867-2

Printed in the United States of America
A-1

To Lynn E. Rose
Bruno's unrelenting Poliinnio

Jove said that the gods had given intellect *and* hands *to man. The* gods had made man *similar to the gods themselves by doing this, and so gave man power over the* other *animals. This* human *power consists in man's being able not only to operate from human sensation as a limit, with its repeated routines. But this human power enabled man to operate from out of human sensation, going beyond these routines, to form newly made natures, newly made methods, newly made logical forms which would reflect the fullest possible range of human intelligence. Without this god-given freedom, to use the fullest possible range of his human intelligence, man would not have the likeness to the gods which the gods did give him. With this fullest range of human intelligence, man can succeed in preserving himself, as god of the earth. When this full, creative, human intelligence becomes idle, it will be frustrated and vain. It will be just as useless as the eye that does not see and the hand that does not grasp. And for this reason,* Providence has determined *that man (as the gods made him) be not in thoughtful reflexion without, at the same time, being activated physically; and that man (as the gods made him) be not in physical action without being thoughtfully reflexive at the same time. This is so, by Providence,* even though it may appear *that a man is engaged only with his hands or is engaged only with his intellect.*

GIORDANO BRUNO
The Expulsion of the Triumphant Beast
London, 1584
Third Dialogue; First Part
Translated by A. Mann Paterson from
Opere Italiane (Gentile)

PREFACE

THE PURPOSE OF THIS BOOK is to point up five main problems which have been responsible for the misunderstanding of the contribution of Francis Bacon to his times and to posterity. First, there is the claim made by scholars that Bacon promised a new method for the natural sciences and then did not deliver it. Second, there is the complete misunderstanding of what Bacon said about "anticipations"; even Fischer and Popper do not understand this. Third, there is the lack of understanding of the constitutive role which the natural philosophers of Italy played in Bacon's encyclopedic achievement. Fourth, the reconstruction of human science as Bacon recommended it needs to be understood as a reformed method of tradition; the sciences (physical and civil) were in dynamic interplay. This was based on the materializing of the metaphysical doctrine of the coincidence of contraries. Cusa wrote it, Bruno materialized it. Fifth, the role of encyclopedists during Bacon's lifetime has not been understood. These men were considered as subversives and collected avant-garde or condemned manuscripts at the risk of their lives. Bacon's faithful labor to keep these ideas alive and in circulation has never been understood. His success in causing much of this brave new thought to be integrated into legitimate cultural pursuit deserves honest recognition.

It has not seemed appropriate to weigh this book down with mountains of footnotes. The chapter on knowledge can be verified in Bacon's aphorisms which are in the *Novum Organum*. They are easy to read. The chapter on government can be verified in the *Advancement of Learning*. Most of the work of Bruno done in England in 1583-5 is available now in English. There is also my previous book on Bruno, *The Infinite Worlds of Giordano Bruno*.

No scholar can do it all. As Bruno pointed out: "It is enough that each man attempt the journey." I have attempted to set the record of Francis Bacon on a more correct path.

The author wishes to acknowledge the encouragement and understanding afforded this long project by Marvin Farber and Lynn E. Rose. Mention should be made of the opportunities afforded the author to discuss this material; William T. Parry, John Abrams and Stillman Drake were helpful in this way.

The theses of this book are my own and the scholars acknowledged should not be held responsible for my views.

I would like to acknowledge the help of Janice Nuzzo, my former student, who worked on the bibliography, Karyn Conlon, who helped with the final typescript, and Elizabeth Morse, who typed the preliminary draft.

Buffalo, New York   ANTOINETTE MANN PATERSON

Also appearing in this Series are the following volumes:

THE INFINITE WORLDS OF GIORDANO BRUNO—Antoinette Paterson
PHENOMENOLOGY, ROLE, AND REASON—Maurice Natanson
THE STRUCTURE OF MORALITY—Hector-Neri Castaneda
THE SELF AND THE WORLD IN THE PHILOSOPHY OF JOSIAH ROYCE—
    Bhagwan Singh
THE FIELD CONCEPT IN CONTEMPORARY SCIENCE—Mendel Sachs
TIME AND METHOD—Ferdinand Gonseth
HUMANISM AND MARX'S THOUGHT—Howard Parsons
THE PHILOSOPHY OF INDIA AND ITS IMPACT ON AMERICAN THOUGHT—
    Dale Riepe
THE AESTHETIC FIELD—Arnold Berleant
THE STRUCTURE OF INDIAN THOUGHT—Ramakant Sinari

CONTENTS

FRANCIS BACON AND SOCIALIZED SCIENCE

INTRODUCTION

I T IS A DIFFICULT TASK to try to determine exactly what Bacon did produce and achieve, and in what field he did make his most crucial contribution; for the many interpreters of Bacon either eulogize him or else hold him in almost complete contempt. The basic positions taken are not for the most part based upon a severely analytical study of Bacon as a member of a particular society, in a particular world crisis, at a particular time. Rather, the writers assume an emotive or patriotic value about Bacon and then proceed to buoy that view with highly selective excerpts from his writings, which they interpret in a highly tenuous way. The patriotic views of the writers throw them into two widely divergent paths: good Bacon and bad Bacon. The same holds for religious bias on the part of the writers. Atheists claim him as their own. Very orthodox Christians claim him also. Ecumenical writers hail him as their chief. Those writers who are anti-papal claim him. And many others hold him as transcending these issues.

Even the age-old strife between the Tudors and the Stuarts creeps into the writings about Bacon. In all of these writings, especially of the seventeenth and eighteenth and nineteenth centuries, the writers assume a bias, and then proceed to prove their bias with little regard for objectivity. For the most part, these writings follow an imprimatur both from the archives and from the other authorities belonging to the same faction; one book after another is a regurgitation of quotes and anecdotes from previously approved volumes.

It is surprising that many books simply collect dust on the shelves and are not even opened. These are the few books that offer a view that has not had the imprimatur of the archive or of some official royal spokesman. For example, Lewis Einstein's *The Italian Renaissance in England* had to have the pages cut before this writer could read it. This happened in both of the two libraries

3

where the book was found. The book was written in 1902, and presents a view not in harmony with the Bacon worshipers or the royal texts. Professors have simply ignored it.

The War of the Roses has not ended. The literature on the Tudor period is neatly divided into the Lancasters and the Yorks. Some writers do not attempt to leave their readers in doubt upon this point. Some writers proceed with elaborate logic, which becomes enmeshed with hair-splitting accounts of the conduct of the monarchs and the court. Most of their evidence, when very carefully sifted, reduces to speculative rationale to support a highly emotional bias which has chosen sides in the ancient feud of the English rulers.

Francis Bacon is enmeshed in this problem. He was a man of the Tudor and the Stuart courts. He was supported by the Crown all of his life for direct and vital service to the court. So was his brother Anthony Bacon, who has been dropped by English historians and students of statecraft.

A decently serious grasp of Bacon's times and work is not possible without a careful study of the Western world at the time in which he operated. This entails a methodological suspension of the present state of the international scene. One cannot start from the present understanding of England, and then proceed to roll back the years. For in this way one is simply following the *national text* that has been constructed layer upon layer from nationalistic and political need as the flailing monarchy sought its balance. The scholarship that proceeds in this way refuses to use all the facts available and provides facts that are missing. In faithfulness to mathematical numbering, these scholars admit that they are operating on the principle that when fact interferes with historical continuity, then the facts must be altered to fit. What is missing here is the final verification with common sense. Claims are made which violate everything we know about human reaction and human need. Claims are made which violate the basic truths about ordinary human life. However, we are offered one book after another filled with the same repetitious anecdotes. One bias has its set of anecdotes, and the other bias has *its* set of anecdotes; when the anecdotes happen to overlap, they are construed in completely different ways. Some of the most scholarly books contain one paragraph after another that are virtually identical with paragraphs in other books.

The archives used by these authors are from the official record offices. Typically, these documents are without dates, or with altered dates; they have some words that are erased and other words that have been added; and they are often of uncertain authorship. Entire spans of time have no records at all, especially at the most crucial points of conflict in the culture.

The tragedy here lies in the maltreatment of those times; the people whose lives created the actual events in Tudor England have not been described from a neutral corner. The tragedy lies also in the childish insistence that these Englishmen must only be known in a way which satisfies the vested interest groups that come immediately after them. Again, their images are mutilated beyond recognition in order that scholars may protect their own feelings about what these people should have been doing and saying at the time.

The earmark of the history of ideas should be its ability to reflect the actual record of human events, and to report them *as they were lived*. Whosoever tampers with these facts from past times obliterates the footprints of men and women and puts in place of them a chartered, theoretical, and completely useless construct, one which intends to condition the young in order that they may approach cultural problems in the manner best suited for making the theoreticians' bias a popular one.

The facts that constitute the Tudor period must be discovered by history. They must not be invented from *a priori* irrationalism. The logic of history must be based upon the descriptive method of the natural sciences, as Bacon himself suggested in his *Advancement of Learning* (*A.L.*, II, ii, 12). An ounce of respect for Francis Bacon, Elizabeth I, etc., would have prohibited the writing of many of the books produced on Tudor England. They are loaded with hundreds of footnotes that the authors feel honor-bound to include but do not integrate. The practice has been to use these kinds of information as the material for what is called the historical novel, and lately many scholars have offered non-formal writings for the "layman" in order to use this material. In this way the scholar hopes to avoid the vicious ridicule of his colleagues for diverging from the "acceptable" script of the academic team. He also avoids acknowledging that he has taken seriously any material outside of the national imprimatur.

I do not feel that Francis Bacon or Elizabeth I need the protection of a guarded, theoretically conventional description. The only acid test employed here will be a neutral re-construction of events in Tudor England and a final test of the work against common sense. By common sense, I mean all the sane insights we have at our disposal about the reactions and needs of human beings in life and under stress.

In this book I have attempted to give an accurate exposition and account of Bacon's work and accomplishments, usually in my words, but frequently in Bacon's own words. Except for indicating which of Bacon's works each section of this book is primarily derived from, however, it has hardly seemed worthwhile to provide documentation for each statement made, since the reader can easily find the relevant passages upon reading the Baconian work in question.

There are many places in Bacon's writings where he is simply repeating points that he has made elsewhere. Sometimes he repeats himself *verbatim*, and sometimes he rewords or rephrases what he has already said. Since Bacon does so often repeat himself and reword himself, the reader should be cautioned that where this book presents direct quotations from Bacon, there are often other passages in Bacon where the same point is made in slightly different words. It has not seemed worthwhile, however, to weight this book down with references sorting out these various sources, since my primary aim has been to present an exposition of what Bacon was doing, and since extensive documentation of the quotations that I have used would distract from, rather than serve that purpose.

At some later date, when Bacon and his work have been evaluated in a realistic and open manner, more material may be seen as his own synthesis of the philosophical systems of this day. The contention that certain works "were begun as far as composition was concerned in 1583" will be ignored. The state of affairs as to the dates on the myriad of papers left in Bacon's collection is beyond serious consideration at this time, mainly because of the outlandish claims made for Bacon by men insistent to use him as the philosophical and scientific symbol of a new method. In this way, claims were made which could not hold up under scrutiny. And then, Bacon became the target of the ensuing abuse as if he himself had made these claims, which he had not.

Therefore, for now, this book will analyze the *Advancement of Learning,* published in 1605; the *Novum Organum,* published in 1620; the *De Augmentis Scientiarum,* published in 1623; and the third edition of the *Essays,* published in 1625. The writer takes the position that the rest of the publishings that were not issued under Bacon's supervision must be re-examined before they can be taken as Bacon's encyclopedic decisions.

Bacon entered Cambridge in 1573 at the age of thirteen. He stayed only two years, and during that time missed an appreciable amount of time due to illness and due to an epidemic of the plague. Bacon earned no formal degree from the school. This is in contrast to Essex, Raleigh, Sydney, and Greville, all of whom completed a structured program of study and were awarded their degrees.

Bacon then entered Grey's Inn, a law school. He did not follow the formal course there, but rather read as he wished and followed the events in the courts as they happened. He was only there about one and one-half years, and then in 1576 he left for Paris.

He was abroad for three years at this time, and the record suggests that he did not travel abroad after that. Bacon was part of the English embassy to the court of France: he was a courtier. He was only sixteen then, and he was allowed to travel through the grand circuit of Europe, which was considered to be the polishing exercise for young potential English courtiers.

For three years after his return to England, he remained inconspicuous at Grey's Inn as a reader in law. Then, as a result of much pressure from Bacon and his mother and his relatives, the Queen named him Utter Barrister at the Inn. Although he walked around in legal robes amongst the students, he was not known to have pleaded any private cases or to have had any noticeable court assignment.

Two years later he obtained a seat in the Commons for Dorsetshire, due to the efforts of his uncle Lord Burleigh, William Cecil, who was Elizabeth's right arm and was her Secretary of State and

Lord Keeper. Two years later he was given the title of a Bencher at the Inn by the Crown. Actually, Bacon was not on the inside of the court as yet and was not a power either in legal circles or in the political arena.

The noticeable change in Bacon's motions in the politics of the court came *only* ιafter the return of his brother Anthony from abroad. Anthony had left England with Francis in 1576 and had also returned home to bury Sir Nicholas Bacon. But Anthony chose "self-banishment" (letter in Birch) and returned to Europe. In spite of his poor health, and in spite of the constant danger from political strife, Anthony refused to come home until 1592. The Queen tried hard to force him to return, but he would not do so. The record appears to suggest that even after his return Anthony refused to go to Elizabeth at the Court even though she frequently asked him to come.

The Queen died a matter of months after Anthony died. This is a considered decision that I have reached after studying the records. The record indicates that Anthony had avoided personal contact with her after his return. Anthony was ill a lot and unable to get about, but one is reminded that when Burleigh was too ill to see the Queen, the Queen went to see Burleigh. Essex House or Grey's Inn was very close to Elizabeth. Perhaps the record of their meeting simply has not survived; the absence of the account should not be treated as absolute proof that they did not see each other. Elizabeth had leaned very heavily upon Anthony's security reports from abroad. It was only through Elizabeth's permission that Anthony's foreign passport was renewed each time that he had insisted upon it.

In addition to gathering political intelligence for Elizabeth, Anthony probably helped Francis gather more general information, not restricted to the political; for this was one of Francis' main projects: the encyclopedic gathering of information. Francis Bacon may indeed be regarded as more a collector than an originator; he admits this in the *Novum Organum* (*N. O.,* I, 116-117):

> And although on some special subjects and in an incomplete form
> I am in possession of results which I take to be far more true and
> more certain and withal more fruitful than those now received (and
> these I have collected into the fifth part of my Instauration), yet I
> have no entire or universal theory to propound. I candidly confess

that the natural history which I now have, whether collected from books or from my own investigations, is neither sufficiently copious nor verified with sufficient accuracy to serve the purposes of legitimate interpretation.

A great deal of what has been passed down to us in the name of Bacon may not, in truth, have been his. For he maintained in his huge estates, at all times, a collection of young intellectuals and writers (Hobbes had been one). Bacon kept these men wined and dined in luxury and clothed in only the highest of fashions. As part of his legal work for the throne, Bacon confiscated estates, which included libraries. His brother Anthony spent thirteen years in France, and Italy, and had the confidence of many significant writers and access to their works. Anthony wrote to Bacon constantly, as he did to the Lord Keeper of England and to the Queen. English scholars and young men of promise were all expected to spend their years after college on tour of France and Italy, where they were to mix with the intellectually elegant. England was a child in these days, a toddler. The Queen realized the challenge involved in order to insure the growth and development of her England. Elizabeth I imported the finest scholars available.

Many of them were Italian Jews from southern Italy, and the finest gentlemen of the Elizabethan court were Italianate or universal men. Some of them were from France; although, with Elizabeth I, the court influence was less French, because of the Mary Stuart problem, and leaned more toward the Italians and Philip II. These two monarchs, Philip II and Elizabeth I, although they warred, were in mutual respect of each other, for many reasons of long standing. He had helped her to the throne. In any case, these men of the "older" cultures were sophisticated gentlemen of long-established savoir-faire in scholarship, domestic government, and international politics.

The Queen was a gifted and highly intellectual monarch, who learned quickly and thoroughly. She was also a very critically thinking and independent monarch who seemed to enter into mature and honorable contracts with the brilliant men she hired for her cabinet. In thirty years, Elizabeth I had pulled England from obscurity to recognition as the mistress of the high seas. She seemed to accomplish this in spite of domestic intrigue rather than because of domestic assistance. In England, the Queen's ascension to the throne had been precarious, and her continuation on the throne remained precarious. Because of the tremendous domestic chaos about her, Elizabeth I chose very sparingly from her own countrymen for confidential advisers. As there were mercenaries in her military, so there was hired expertise from abroad in her court. England's plight at this time is not to be seen as unusual. Most monarchs were faced with the same precarious conditions. But England, blazing a trail in political Deism, was alone with many peculiar problems of loyalty and disloyalty.

Much has been written about the romantic episodes in the Queen's life. Most of it seems to be legend, intended to present Elizabeth as powerful, as seminal. She lived, as a monarch, in a monarch's world and needed to create images and roles that would be understood as connoting power. Actually, from a serious study of Elizabeth, one can only come away with the record of a keenly intellectual and inventive genius who suffered no illusions of where her responsibilities were. Elizabeth saved England in those days, a lone monarch with an acuteness and sensitivity to facts that have been hardly equaled since. It is a mistake and a distortion of the facts to give the credit to Bacon or anyone else. Elizabeth never gave Bacon any crucial power to decide England's destiny. When James I seemed to be forced to do so, because of Bacon's experience in the Commons and his eagerness to serve, the result was unfortunate chaos. This was because Bacon did not have any powerful political caucus behind him.

Bacon's allegiances were always eclectic and changed with the "signs" as he read them.

CHAPTER ONE

METHOD OF
LEARNING RE-FORMED

1. Regulated Observation
2. Corrected Anticipation
3. Legitimate Interpretation
4. Copernicus and Bacon's
   Socialized Science

1.

Regulated Observation

THIS ENTIRE CHAPTER is an account of Francis Bacon's collected and edited rendition of the "re-formed intellect" and "re-formed senses" in the natural sciences. These concepts, especially clear in Cusanus, Leonardo da Vinci, Giordano Bruno, and Galileo, had gained much ground. Bacon was devoted in his attempt to fit the "re-formed intellect" and "re-formed senses" into systematic inquiry.

Eucatalepsia was Bacon's word for the scientific balance of "mature suspension of judgment" and "posita juris" (deposits of reason). Man had a double duty: to exonerate his own reasonable power and to support the method of tradition in order to guarantee the advancement of natural sciences and the reasonable power of existential human life. (*A.L.*, II, xxi, 2, 6; xxiii, 6; xxv, 1, 3, 8).

Human reality for Bacon could be shaped by human power. Human power had two fountains, which had to be harnessed. One was nature as a whole (*natura naturans, N.O.*, II, preface), with all of its latent laws. Bruno used this phrase. The other was nature as particular physical things that manifested those laws of latent configurations. For Bacon, as for Bruno, the irony lay in the brutal fact that human power would not be able to harness nature and her dual aspects *unless human power first harnessed itself and its own dual aspect* (namely, conditioned volition and re-formed intellect). Human nature had been entangled by the net of social superstition. Thereby, neither the emotions nor the intellect of man had been able to develop a properly *balanced* system of natural or social science.

The proper system would be a balance of the full range of human power and would provide a platform for the good life and the good state by means of re-formed science of existence. In the case of the social sciences, the manipulation and use of the simple natures or particles of the society would be based upon the same method as that of the natural sciences. Correct anticipation of the law of these simple natures must be a result of an inductive foreknowledge.

Bacon reflected the mood of his times, which were boiling with the emerging technology and capitalism. Existential men were inheriting the earth, and they were *not* meek! Bacon suggests that to imitate nature we must discover and then interpret the hidden law of its operation. We must do a good imitation of nature and work as nature does, with a view to works. Our aim must be to superimpose a new set of works upon the natural works. We have a man-centered aim to be satisfied. This will entail inventing what is useful from nature's works.

Most of our notions are cloaked in words and so remain ill-defined. We need "an intellectual operation" which can derive precise notions from axioms, with the aim of penetrating nature. The senses are the source of the axioms; that is, the axioms are derived from the senses. We must start with the particular things and proceed with steps of penetration which elucidate the steps that are prior in the natural order.

In Bacon as in Bruno, the hands need aids also. Both the hands and the understanding work together and must have the proper tools to do their job well. Both the understanding and the hands can take apart and put together again. The mind cuts with the blade of reason, and the hand uses the blade of metal. Nature generates and corrupts things, and nature does all of this from within the thing.

As Bruno says it (in *De Immenso,* I, ii, 275):

> Naturaque sit rationi
> Lex; non naturae, ratio.
> Nature must be law for
> reason; not reason for nature.

Bacon notes that nature alone increases works. The mechanical arts are thriving because they remain in the womb of nature. Their laws are still hidden in the folds of nature. The systems of opinions and doctrines are severed from any natural womb, and their laws are not from nature. Therefore they do not thrive in a productive way, through works. These dogmas seem dedicated to despair, as man is encouraged not to allow the senses their authority at all.

It is no different in the arts or in public affairs. They too have been torn from the womb of nature and from the natural sciences. Mathematics and medicine are the rulers of natural science. We have not had a whole man working. Monks in cells and gentlemen in castles are all we have had. Because the mechanical experimentation aims at producing fruits rather than light, it does not produce the needed axioms. We need state channels in the natural sciences. We need to order experience according to fixed laws. This calls for a new system. Literacy is a must in the natural sciences. Records must be kept in the courts of experiment. Invention is not approached only by record, though; one needs also to use his hands, to perform lawful physical trials. The written record is the blend of both thought and hands.

As in Bruno's *Spaccio,* Bacon describes how the goal of the natural philosophers should be service to human welfare. Human life should be endowed with new discoveries which will give the human race more powers. The power of simple human experience should be used in order to accomplish this. Induction proceeds from the accidental experience to the prescribed experiment. Long observation of particulars and experiments can in no way injure the senses. Bacon laments the paradox that the material globe has opened up and that the intellectual globe of man has remained closed. As in Bruno, one could say that the ancients are newer than we are, although they are older in time. Time should have some rights, and time is the author of authors. It is sad that authors turn into authority from time to time and time passes in the dark. Truth is the daughter of time and not the daughter of authority.

Bacon understood the re-formed mood of the whole man. He writes that one does not have fruit just because he has books, because books can suffocate the truth. Where there is no utility, there cannot be said to be truth. Talkers and writers and dreamers parade themselves as perfections before the people. They promise them the prolongation of life, retardation of age, alleviance of pain, the repairing of natural defects. A despair sets in which sharply reduces the possibilities of human experience.

The world is not to be treated as a slave to thought, nor should thought be treated as slave to words. Here, we are reminded of the Bruno quotation given above. On the river of time much floats down to us by the very virtue of its flimsy nature. Words and words and no works are what makes for the flimsy nature of the systems. For Bacon, both philosophy and religion are to be judged by works, as in Bruno also. The systems of opinions increase always, but they do not increase works. If one contemplates and comes up with the idea of cause, he has come up with the idea of rule for operation. In order to make the concept of cause a useful one, the student must use aids for his contemplative activity. The understanding must adhere to some basic rules of logic. The hands are no different from the understanding in this regard, for Bacon. On the other hand, the fact that the senses must observe the experiment will insure that the mind of the observer will not fly to unwarranted claims. If it were not for the experiment, the mind would not stop in its flight and there would be a dizzy ascent to heights, unchecked by the restrictions of the reason. What is needed are forms or laws of actual operation in nature, and not forms or laws which are mere figments of the human mind.

Bacon reminds us that words are not replacements for instances. If the instance is left behind, one might find himself in the plight of the very fast runner who has taken the wrong turn and whose speed is totally defeating him. The most worthwhile approach to a just and ordered reason is a good steady hand and a good steady understanding. Practice with the tools will assure this steadiness. The experiments of the natural scientists should not be experiments of fruits but they should be experiments of light. One should not go after the thing itself but should start inquiry through the particular to Bacon's methodological "tables" and from the "tables" to the middle axioms. From the axiom an experiment of descent will be suggested which will be of a general nature. Natural philosophers should use only sound notions. The tools of reason are not the tools of faith. Render to faith only what belongs to faith. Natural philosophers who use the Scriptures as the tool of natural philosophy are not sound at all. Furthermore, the distinction between natural and violent motion is not a sound one. Natural motion is violent motion. Atoms and unformed matter are not sound notions because they are not able to improve human welfare. Natural philosophers should not rob the senses of their authority. The natural philosophers should aid the senses and help correct them rather than dismiss their role. Bacon is clearly not an advocate of extreme rationalism. And yet, as we read him, Bacon deplored the eager empirics who used "trial and error" alone in the hunt for quick, pragmatic results.

The unskilled proceed to investigate the nature of a thing through that thing. We all know that the nature of a thing is not made manifest through the particulars. Natural science depends on the power of men to draw out the latent laws of nature, and this power must be born of a just and orderly union of the re-formed senses and the re-formed reason. The reason alone cannot form axioms that will give new particulars. The reason must bite into the material of nature through higher sense and particulars. The reason cannot bite into empty air and sew a strong garment. When new particulars are suggested by the higher axioms and are then discovered by careful and lawful descent from those higher axioms, we must re-form our experience in light of our new particulars. Our sense axioms will now change, as we proceed from the new particulars to the formation of higher axioms.

First principles should never entail a confrontation with civil law, which is based on natural law. If the first principles are of true laws of nature they will enter into the just and orderly procedure quietly and surely as they fill obvious needs and increase human power. Full testing of public middle axioms involves a socialized team devising the scientifically useful experiment. When the re-formed senses observe the legitimate experiment, the full range of possibility for human existential future can be demonstrated.

In Aphorism I of *N.O.*, II, Bacon uses the phrase that Bruno used, "natura naturans":

> Datae autem naturea formam,
> sive differentiam veram, sive
> naturam naturantem. . . .

Bacon writes in these lines that given natures have a natural source from which they emanate the way they do: find the law of natura naturans and manipulate the given natures from their source. There would be no end to possible human invention in the future then. But Bacon says that we will have to start the job being satisfied with studying manifest generation and motion of concrete bodies through their manifest efficient causes and their manifest material for discovery of latent process. In this way also, we can look for latent configurations in bodies at rest. Through comparative physical experiments, the simple natures involved in them may be learned. In this way, we proceed slowly and pursue the natural science through the re-formed common sense. We do not start out by trying to penetrate this "natura naturans".

2.

CORRECTED ANTICIPATION

THE CONCEPT OF ANTICIPATION in Francis Bacon has not been well understood. This is partially the fault of the manner in which Bacon tried to stay within the context of his culture and avoid the problem that Bruno and Galileo encountered. Actually Bacon was trying to re-word these teachings in order that the study of nature would appear to remain respectably within the societal expectations of his own times. When Bacon rejects anticipation, he always does so in a qualified way. He describes exactly the kind of anticipation that he finds to be without merit, namely, the anticipation that does not rest upon methodological observation.

The conclusions of human reason as ordinarily applied in matters of nature, I call for the sake of distinction Anticipations of Nature (as a thing rash or premature). That reason which is elicited from facts by a just and methodical process, I call Interpretation of Nature. (*N.O.*, I, xxvi)

Anticipations are a ground sufficiently firm for consent, for even if men went mad all after the same fashion, they might agree one with another well enough. (*N.O.*, I, xvii)

For the winning of assent, indeed, anticipations are far more powerful than interpretations, because being collected from a few instances, and those for the most part of familiar occurrence, they straightway touch the understanding and fill the imagination; whereas interpretations, on the other hand, being gathered here and there from very various and widely dispersed facts, cannot suddenly strike the understanding; and therefore they must needs, in respect of the opinions of the time, seem harsh and out of tune, much as the mysteries of faith do. (*N.O.*, I, xxviii)

In sciences founded on opinions and dogmas, the use of anticipations and logic is good; for in them the object is to command assent to the proposition, not to master the thing. (*N.O.*, I, xxix)

19

Though all the wits of all the ages should meet together and combine and transmit their labors, yet will no great progress ever be made in science by means of anticipations; because radical errors in the first concoction of the mind are not to be cured by the excellence of functions and subsequent remedies. (*N.O.*, I, xxx)

Bacon writes that spontaneous or accidental anticipation cannot be trusted, even though it may sometimes lead to a successful demonstration of some pet hunch of ours about natural objects. For these results are not planned as an integral part of a well defined body of organized knowledge, and may actually not be good for anything else but the enhancing of a reputation or the supporting of some superstition. In this way, the study of nature remains tied to superstition and to the precocious whims of totally undisciplined men who are not looking for works at all, but are merely playing with their imaginations.

Bacon repeatedly states that anticipation can and must be left behind and that—*before anticipation is released*—a serious researcher guides his senses and wipes free his understanding faculty by reaching for physical aids, such as written tables of comparison. "Eucatalepsia" is Bacon's word for methodological suspension of anticipation. The tables of comparison are the aids which help sustain this eucatalepsia. The physical objects or processes that are to be studied must be put under *regulated observation* by the proper adjustment of the researcher's powers of sense; his observation will henceforth be of the sort that is generated by the methodology itself (see Bruno's "logical observation" in the *De Immenso*). A *shift* must be made from the anthropomorphic, culturally-conditioned observer to the *regulated observer*. A regulated observer will be one who will *suspend anticipation* (eucatalepsia) until he has observed the phenomenon through the eyes and ears of a *pre-established plan*, a plan that has been publicly designed by researchers with the declared goal and aim of discovering a utilitarian fragment of knowledge. This regulated observer will know exactly what he is looking for and why he is looking for it.

One of the most central expressions in the work of Giordano Bruno was "regolato sentimento". Sentimento meant the passions, the affective nature of man. Sentimento was that aspect of man which responded the best to measures of conditioning by the culture. As Bruno pointed out: patriotism, family ties, habits of worship and idiosyncracies of one's person all made man vulnerable to manipulation which dictated the emotional anticipations of a man. In Bruno, sentiment had to be *gently protracted* into socially responsible patterns, but not patterns which caused the intellectual "wings" that man had to become diseased. In the *De Immenso,* Bruno used this analogy. Man could only move in science if he steered with intellectual "wings" which were physically empowered (through their integrated physical structure) by a healthy body. Scientific man (as an eagle in flight) must have his intellectual "wings" coordinated with the rest of his system. The reasonable faculty, lodged in the head, fused the imaginative sentimental with the intellectual energies and eye-images. This faculty of reason then dissects this fused image, with the faculty of its own eye. Philo had said that the mind was both glue and knife. This is how the faculty of reason is infused with power from the sentiment and the intellect.

This regulated sentiment of Bruno's appears in Bacon as the *anticipation of the mind* as opposed to the anticipation from the mere human nature acting out of conscience or other conditioned state. Bacon wrote that there will be two fountains of knowledge, neither one taking away from the other, each with its own stream (administration); two comparably knowledgeable kinds of thinkers, rational empirics and empirical rationalists. As kinfolk, they are neither alien nor inimicable to each other, but in mutual succor they are of one rationale and of one duty; then, at long last, human judgment will do other than merely tend familiar knowledge: it will be discovering new knowledge. For those who choose the former as they admire it more (due to lack of interest, intellectual power or the necessary time for activity outside of social life) he offers his best wishes for their success. But if men who are not content with the former method, which does not penetrate into nature, would like to follow him, Bacon invites this kind of man to join him. Bacon promises that this other way does not merely spend time in verbal argument or fantastic conjectures. Bacon explains that he has given the new system a name. It is the latter system mentioned above, and it has to do with discovery (inveniendi). This system of discovery has two paths, or kinds of judgments.

Bacon calls one of the paths of the system of discovery, AN-TICIPATIONS OF THE MIND. The other path of the system of discovery is called, INTERPRETATION OF NATURE. Bacon says that even though he is primarily concerned with finding the truth in natural science, he is concerned that his new system of discovery be presented to the most uninitiated man in a gentle and well-timed manner. Bacon calls for persuasion of the human spirit toward change (Preface to *N.O.*).

Most writers who deal with this passage translate "mentis" and "animos" as both meaning "mind". I do not. It is the anticipations of the "mentis" that must be in control of the anticipations from human "animos". Note that "ad animos hominum" is what takes on the persuasions of others. For Bacon, the corrected anticipations of the human mind were ones that switched their frame of reference from the habitual disposition of the individual man to the frame of reference of an impersonal and ordered cosmos. When the anticipations were spontaneous, they were from the Idols. They were from the *nature* of *man* as it is without intellectual reformation. Therefore the anticipations from the nature of men had to be transformed into the anticipations from the *mind of man*. This was an "intellectual operation" and involved a suspension of habit.

> If a man will begin with certainties
> he shall end in doubts; but if he will
> be content to begin with doubts, he
> shall end in certainties. (*A.L.*, I, v, 8)

Here, again, Bacon calls for eucatalepsia, "mature suspension of judgment" (*A.L.*, I, v, 8), which I take to be his anticipations of "mentis". "Mentis" in Bacon is an aware human intelligence. When the scientist starts out in this mood, his Interpretations of Nature will be true and certain, as they will be based upon properly introduced evidence from regulated observation. These legitimately judicial and sound *decisions* are handed down as *legitimate precedents* to be followed, until they are legitimately over-ruled after a due and properly conducted new trial, a trial that exonerates new evidence that has been brought to bear upon the petition.

This is the "regolato sentimento" of Giordano Bruno. For Bruno the passions and emotions of the heart must be re-formed and rechanneled into the new forms; this operation is to be based upon the power that man has to be critical and intellectual and universal in his reasoning. Both knowing and feeling are important powers of the human organism, but the proper use of these powers mandates the proper proportion of them for specific tasks. When one is trying to understand nature, Bruno wrote that man must lose those of his "habits" that are based on the early teachings he received "in his father's house". As with the Stoics, the scientific disposition must be a universal one, and not driven through the local channels of the human organism alone. Rather, this local current should flow into the oceanic pool of universal mind. In "moto del cuore" men served their conscience, which was constructed from the habits of religion, personal honor, family tradition, and country loyalties. To work in science with the "regolato sentimento", one must write prescriptions based on uniformity from correct measurement and correct logical law and order. In this way the "regolato sentimento" put *balance* into the use of the common sense forms and the intellectual forms that man created and lived by. As noted, translators of Bacon's Latin use the word "mind" for both. Bacon used the word "mentis" in one place and the word "animos" in the other. Bacon read the Romans. Virgil uses this distinction between the animos (as undifferentiated soul) and the mentis (as intelligent soul). It is my position that this passage in Bacon is *crucial* to the understanding of what Bacon was actually saying. It does not help anyone to ignore Bacon's distinctions as he makes them.

Bacon writes that the science of physical bodies and physical processes is inaugurated from the utilitarian appropriation of nature. Bacon sees nothing wrong in the *utilitarian* anticipation of nature; in fact, that is exactly what he wants. The researcher must replace the Idols with a *new set of predispositions* that are not rooted in the scholastic and social habits prevalent in his time. This new set of predispositions is to be constructed from shifting one's frame of reference from the human to the cosmic world. The conventional manner of observation has now been completely set aside, and this dilated regulated observation of the physical experiment (which has been designed as an integrated search for a specific understanding) will enable the researcher to observe things he never would have been able to notice as long as he was bound to spontaneous observation from the Idols.

Bacon wrote that there were two ways of doing natural science. He thought that he had acknowledged the places of both rationalism and empiricism in natural science. The both of them were to be trimmed down to legitimate methodology. One could reduce the rationalist's axiom to sense perception, but this was very difficult to do, and the time was not ripe for that. It would be better, with the present state of affairs and in the light of the past and present abuses of this method, to proceed from the empirical route, *although in a re-formed way*. If empirical attempts were not allowed to be unruly, and if the fruits aimed at were publicly seen to be aimed at the good for the state, then natural science could prosper in his time. Therefore, physical aids would accompany the senses as the senses were put to work on pre-established research designs that did not climb in their aim very far above the common sense experience. Little by little, but surely, and with stability, the man of natural science could accumulate and *write down* his findings. Researchers working from this amassed data could continue to design physical experiments that followed in logical order. In this way, natural scientists would reach some middle axioms from which they could make out the borderline of a more general nature. The more general nature would be explored just as methodologically as was the lower field, which was between the regulated observation and the middle axiom. In this way the topmost axiom would be a long time in being elicited; and time is the parent of truth. We should move as nature does, so slowly that the changes are hardly discernible.

Bacon repeatedly holds that there should never be a confrontation between natural sciences and the government. Scientific findings should slip in quietly and with complete ease, since the times and the knowledge for those times should be in harmony. Although many felt in Bacon's time that doomsday had arrived, and that human life had hit a new low, Bacon did not agree. He sounds cautiously like Bruno when he speaks about the future and the next generations to come. Bacon writes that instead of doomsday those times were a new dawn. Greece and Rome had been the first two great periods, and now this was the third new world.

It is very difficult to study Bacon's works, because he seems to contradict himself so much. But he had to be very careful about what he said. He could not appear to be atheistic or agnostic. If he did, then his loyalty to the throne of England would be under suspicion, because the monarch sat on that throne by virtue of his selection by God to be the vicar of the Divine on earth. Therefore, Bacon had to be a Christian. He could not appear to be recommending that change and innovation should be called for in the civil government. Bacon states all the time that the natural scientist must have utilitarian goals before him for the welfare of the people. But he had to explain that, too. He had to explain that underfed and disloyal people made poor soldiers and poor subjects, and that the king who ruled animals did not rule well. This was in the Philonic tradition and was really very old and was being recalled from the earlier Christian era when the rule of churchmen and nobles was much more altruistic than it was in these days of Bacon's. He was treading on dangerous ground and he knew it. Therefore, he writes as a hard natural philosopher in one passage and seems to take it back in another. He denounces rationalism in one place, and then explains how to make it respectable, because it could be a legitimate method. He does the same with empiricism.

In one place he says that he will not discuss politics. In another place he slips in a few choice words and observations. It appears that as he got older and especially after he became Lord Chancellor, he began to be more bold and less prudent. As I understand it from close study of his life, work, and collected publishings, Bacon wanted to disseminate the best of the thinkers and scientists of his times in such a way that the publishings could be widely read. He did not want his collections burned. They represented a lifetime of reflective editorial work and very large sums of money, year in and year out, which he had had to beg and grab any way he could.

Bacon almost seems to try to follow the style of the Scriptures by writing in short, aphoristic style or very short narrative. He makes a point of saying that he writes in this fashion because he would dispell the idea that he knew it all. Rather, he was bent upon presenting some cloaked and enigmatic suggestions for men of reflective nature to entertain. If he wrote bluntly in one place, then he would write just as bluntly in another place to suggest a contrary point.

Now we can understand why Bacon says that he has found a system which balanced both the empirical method and the rational method into "an integrated logical operation" for natural science. Bacon simply did put "weights on the wings" because he wanted the system used and not suppressed. Therefore, modified in its flight to *suit the times,* this system could accomplish a lot. The re-formed religion in England, although very strict about men remaining "under the throne", would allow anything at all which would give the struggling nation existential prowess and power. Remember, and I repeat this a lot: for Bacon (who spoke from observing the existential realities), *truth was the daughter of time and not of authority.* But this was no challenge such as Bruno made. This was a reminder to re-formed minds that time would eventually win out over authority, and so prudence was the most effective posture for the welfare of the state. In the *Spaccio* (Imerti), Bruno says that Truth should not travel around without her two constant companions, Providence and Prudence. These two virtues are connected to each other. Bruno adds that they may have to link up with Dissimulation if necessity of the social situation demands it. Bacon agreed.

In Bacon, operations and mechanics should be seen as preceding the contemplative, because legitimate laws of nature can only be induced from the material and efficient manifestations of physical bodies, taken as generalized. Otherwise, contemplation is not disposed toward human welfare or usefulness and proceeds without the necessary common-sense guides. Again, man can then operate freely toward the remaking of the world around him to serve human uses for human planning, because man can imitate nature. When man understands the latent rules, then he can appropriate them and put the materials and efficacities in nature to work. For Bacon, natural materials and fittings will then be at the disposal of the kind of bodies man plans to make. Man becomes the con-creator of his universe. In the *De Monade,* Bruno says man is the "co-operator with nature".

Bacon wrote that knowing the laws of nature enables man to

touch the deeper boundary of things and embrace the unity of nature. Through the laws of nature man can see through the material and efficient differences which bodies manifest and can see the latent relationships between bodies. Once man sees the latent relations between bodies, he can then use this rule of relatedness to create any body he wants to create. From the laws of nature, *latent* natures can actually be deduced. In this way, more and more of the *latent* natures will be discovered.

Therefore, natural scientists for Bacon might have to use the *camouflage* of empiricism to keep the societal powers from the fear that they are replacing the Deistic highest axioms for the explanation of reality. Bacon was willing to do this in natural science as well as in social science. Bruno was not willing that all men should be forced to do this as a rule or as the only legitimate way. For Bruno the door had to be left open so that each scientific man could apply his re-formed method inductively or deductively. The ultimate axiom of the natural scientist should be respected. The need for faith in religion for some people could be respected at the same time, for Bruno.

For Bacon, physics should deal with the common and ordinary course of nature and not with the eternal and fundamental laws of nature. Physics should deal with the efficient causes, the matter of the latent process, and the problem of the latent configuration. The latent processes of nature are the hidden mechanics of nature. The practical aspect of physics would be the actual mechanics that imitate the hidden mechanics of nature. The theoretical part of physics would be to design the actual mechanics in complete imitation of the hidden mechanics in nature.

In Bacon, when the fact can be operated upon with the five common senses, this should be done. We should be doing an anatomy on the physical bodies in nature, just as we do on human bodies. The anatomy on animals and humans is done with physical instruments. The anatomy on other physical bodies must be done with reason. As in the Philonic tradition, the mind glues and cuts. Physical instruments can be used as helpers. Experiments can be used to help. There must also be a comparison with other bodies and a reduction to simple natures and to the laws of these simple natures. Inquiry into nature is best when it begins with physics

and ends with mathematics. There are some operations such as
those on astronomy which are *mere knowing operations.* The fact
itself cannot be operated upon. One must depend on the primary
and universal axioms concerning simple natures or qualities, such
as magnetism and spontaneous rotation. Metaphysics has to do
with the fundamental and eternal law of nature which is essential
to the mechanical laws hidden in nature. "A subdivision of metaphysics is magic." Bacon uses the word magic and emphasizes "the
broadness of its ways."

Bacon said that metaphysics "opens broad roads to human
power" because it looks to "what is eternal and unchanging in
nature." In order to know an object in this way Bacon held that
the object would have to be studied through the data gleaned.
This data would be gathered from studying the object through its
generation, its motions, and its operations. Its operations would be
designed manipulations according to prior classification and comparison. These operations would be tied to observable demonstrations which were always understandable to the common senses of
the trained scientist. Bacon described his method in this way: to
form axioms from experience we proceed from senses to memory
to reason. We need written tables for comparison and classifica-
tions and to reason upon, so that the understanding has a guide
and a guard. Anticipations unguarded by lawful induction from
physical demonstrations are dangerous. Bacon described as "false
assumptions" the notions which proceeded from the incommen-
surable to the commensurable, from surds to rational quantities,
from the infinite to the finite. Therefore he wrote "atoms, vacuum,
unchanging matter, real particles such as really exist are all false
assumptions."

Bacon teaches that the aim of human power is to generate a new
nature upon a given body and thereby transform that concrete
body. Human power works through human knowing. Knowledge
is attained by the human through the study of the material and
efficient aspects of a given body. The aim of human knowledge
is to discover the law of the latent processes and configurations of
the given body. This is the form of the given body. Knowledge has
to do with existing forms and through them can discover the latent
form of the given body. These latent forms are laws of nature. By

virtue of human power, men can transform bodies and generate new natures upon them. These new natures are based squarely upon the laws of nature which have been gleaned through the material and efficient aspects by the physical bodies through the work of human knowing.

These new natures are utilitarian natures. The body now has been transformed into a useful force for human society. Essentially this is what human power and human knowledge is all about for Bacon: the transformation of blind cosmic force into force that is, from the human frame of reference, utilitarian. Theory of knowledge and its operations is based upon the explanation and analysis of the fixed laws in nature as given, laws which determine the purely individual acts performed by individual bodies. "There are no final causes in nature because these fixed laws, purely individual acts, and individual bodies are all that exist in nature." For the kingdom of man as opposed to the kingdom of nature the case is different. Here, final cause can be a useful concept.

It is not enough to know efficient and material causes. We need to know the law which embraces the unity of nature. If we know the laws of nature we can detect and bring to life things never before thought about. The discovery of true and real genus is the result of knowing how to convert the given nature into another nature which is convertible with it, and through this interpretive nature we can anticipate a more general nature. This more general nature is clearly marked off by the limitation of the interpretive nature we have arrived at. This interpretive nature is barely apart from the given nature and is easily converted to it. It is useful and therefore truest. The ascent to more and more perfect axioms will be slow, but the ascent must be guided at each step by the acid test of usefulness and convertibility to the given natures with which the axioms must be usefully expressed.

Nature is not unruly, for Bacon. The law accompanies nature as the useful accompanies the true. Nature is never without works and wastes no effort because it is lawful and in order. Each natural thing is inseparable from the law of nature. We cannot have any natural things at all which are without the law of their natural organization. If we can understand the more general laws of nature, then we can deduce the given natures which constitute particular things. In this way, we will be able to notice things that have previously gone unnoticed. *This corrected observation is legitimatized anticipation of nature.* Human experience will then be enriched because it will not be chained to idols. The reasonable faculty in man is the blade with which he can dissect the composite physical things into their latent laws.

Known natural laws draw a limit upon more general, unknown nature. In this way, natural law carves out real genus. In this way theory of knowledge can have a discovered nature which is convertible with the given nature. Natural law, as understood by men through the material and mechanical manipulation of physical bodies, can deduce general given nature which is in many different *things*. Furthermore, natural law, as described above, can deduce general nature which is in many different *natures*. This general nature is known in common sense in a popular way, although the laws which it hides are not known at all.

The method Bacon was trying to teach was that system which would superinduce qualities from one given body into another given body. This could only be done through the knowledge of the laws of the qualities being used. Qualities were simple natures. A collection of simple natures was a given body. If the laws of collection were discovered for any given body, and the laws of the qualities which made up that collection were also known, then this given body could be dismantled and re-arranged at will. If two given bodies were so well known they could both be dismantled and their qualities exchanged to alter the nature of their collection of qualities. In this way, Bacon thought that transmutation of metals was possible.

In summary, it is my decision that Bacon clearly saw human anticipation of nature as a dual power. It could be attached to fantasy and superstition, or it could be channeled into an external, physical experimental setup, and designed, as a result of long, recorded, comparative, and charted observations that used both agreement of cases and non-agreement of cases and the tables of presence, essence, etc.

3.

LEGITIMATE INTERPRETATION

B ACON WAS A LAWYER. His method of interpretation of nature was simply the transfer of legal rigor to the courtroom of nature. Animal anticipation (Idols of men) must be suspended in favor of corrected anticipations submitted to rules of evidence. The Italian philosophers of nature wrote of the "Great Books of Nature". Bacon would write of the "Great Petition by the Kingdom of Man to the Kingdom of Nature" (which was the Kingdom of God).

The "intellectual operation" that Bacon called for and named as "induction" was the legitimate "drawing out" of latent natural process as *law* of nature. The legitimacy of any claim that man would put to nature must be tried according to strict rules of evidence. If the human claim was disproved by legitimate trial, according to rules of evidence, man must, by a rigorous intellectual operation, grant the loss of his petition.

Bacon did not see mathematics as the instrumental language of methodological observation which would be based on a theoretical ground. Methodological or contrived observation apart from physical paraphernalia was rejected by him. Yet, he called for more than the descriptive method, which he felt merely dealt with the accidental characteristics of any phenomenon. This emphasis on the accidental, non-critical properties of things he thought was a result of the Idols of Mankind. It became a practice because of the habit of feeling secure about grouping things according to their resemblances. This habit led to concentration upon very narrow characteristics and tended to produce generalizations which were not well founded; they were based upon narrow experimentation, tied to human whim. Bacon felt that differences were more revealing than similarities. Distinctions were primary clues to the essen-

31

tial nature of a phenomenon. *A thing's singularity pointed to its (the magnet's) unique configuration or structure.* Generalizations about this should be based upon middle axioms after study also of the similarity of cases *where magnets did not work* and should not be based on grouping together only particular events where they did work. In this way, generalizations would be comprehensively and continuously based on the natural laws elicited from physical experiment, rather than being based on the mere aspect of raw observation of similarities between particular physical events. Well-rounded, or many-sided, regulated observations of particular events were the raw material for legitimate, sound interpretation of nature.

Interpretations of nature proceed from just and orderly reasoning and lead to utilitarian anticipation of nature. These utilitarian anticipations must be tested, for although they readily gain our assent they, too, may be all wrong. This is crucial to keep in mind because anticipations are a much stronger force than interpretations, and we must insist upon the just and orderly anticipation rather than the favorite. In this way, our interpretation of nature will provide us with new man-made natures which will be based on the laws of nature.

Bacon believed that both the method of searching for latent process and the method of searching for latent configurations could be productive if they were tied to matter. Latent process was materially continuous but not visible to us. It could be known by analogy through rigorously doing quantitative analysis of natural motion and operations under regulated observation. Latent configuration was a cluster of simple natures which constituted the composite object that appeared in nature to us. These composite objects had to undergo manipulations or tortures, devised methodologically, to wrest the strategy of the troop of simple natures that composed it.

For Bacon, a body was a troop or collection of simple natures. The challenge was to deduce the latent nature of the physical body through the discovery of the law which governs this troop of simple natures. They could be considered as soldiers who have been mobilized according to a strategy in order to complete a designated piece of work. It is our task to illuminate that strategy through the study of the effects which are manifest to us. Proceeding from compound bodies as they are in nature, we can be concerned with latent process. This is the study of motion and operations of nature through material and efficient causes that have been made manifest to our senses. This was the preferable system for the times, Bacon believed.

Every natural action depends on things that are infinitely small and that do not strike our senses (*N.O.*, II, vi). Bacon's twenty-seventh kind of prerogative instances, Instances of Magic, have to do with "minima".

> Whether there be any mode of changing bodies per minima (as they call it) and of transposing the subtler configurations of matter (a thing required in every sort of transformation of bodies) so that art may be enabled to do in a short time that which nature accomplishes by many windings, is a point on which I have at present no sure indications. And as in matters solid and true I aspire to the ultimate and supreme, so do I forever hate all things vain and tumid, and do my best to discard them. (*N.O.*, II, li)

Bacon seems publicly to reject these minima of Bruno's. He calls them magic, although he has not rejected use of the notion of "simple natures" too small to strike our senses. I hold that this use of the "per minima" by Bacon alludes to Bruno, as did the use of "natura naturans" in Aphorism I in the second book of the *Novum Organum*. Therefore, he had to classify these "minima" as "magic". Vanini had met the executioner in 1619, about the time that Bacon was publishing this. Bacon could not quote Bruno.

However, Bacon proceeds in the style of Bruno's "regolato sentimento", and calls it "anticipatio mentis". Bacon says we must proceed in such a way that these minima can strike our understanding. The method which we must use is one of corrected anticipation. Anticipation which has been controlled through a preparation of the understanding with a natural history. This natural history will not be written from gossip and despair and fear. This natural history will be a collection and recording of natural experience and experiment which is not opinion but has been perfected with sound reason, based upon physical events unmixed with anything that cannot be justified in nature. Regulated method in science will enable natural history to interpret nature.

Natural history will be the studies of natural generation, motion and operation, from effects. Latent natural process can be followed by the reason as long as the reason does not separate itself from the given particular bodies in nature. Reason must penetrate these physical bodies but only by hanging fast to the material and efficient causes and effects of that physical body. This work must begin with physics and end with mathematics. "The method of speculation which starts with surds and proceeds to rational quantities is not to be trusted."

Bacon held that through disciplined study of natural things, the reason will be geared to the fullness of and the regularity of natural law. Human reason should be empowered by the impersonal, non-human forces of raw intelligence unfettered by narrow physical acquaintance of chance and accident. Bacon never realized that he had drawn a deductive model of raw intelligence when he purged the human thinker of his Idols. Bacon asked for methodological theoretical observation of phenomena while he criticized the rationalists. He insisted upon resting the edifice of knowledge upon the particular events which were provoked from manipulation of physical things according to a predetermined model of physical operations. Yet he criticized the empiricist who based knowledge upon a model of simple observation of physical operations.

At first look, Bacon appears to be hopelessly confused and to be in complete contradiction with himself. But let us take a second look at what he is saying. Casual observation cannot be trusted. It is spontaneous. One cannot allow spontaneous observation to report a thing. One must be *aware* that one is going to observe an event for a certain methodological purpose. The Idols must be set aside, and one must deliberately observe an event in a neutered manner. One does not observe phenomena as a social being, a civilized being, or a citizen. One turns oneself into raw intelligence, and observes what is there, with no regards for conventions. Then one proceeds to use both induction and deduction, but in a reformed way. Bacon says in the Preface of the *Instauratio* (1620):

> . . . I have established for ever a true and lawful marriage between
> the empirical and the rational faculty, the unkind and ill-starred
> divorce and separation of which has thrown into confusion all the
> affairs of the human family.

One is able to concentrate on distinctions not ever noticed

before. This affirmation has been distilled by the boiling away of similarities. When the long comparative operations (which have been guarded by the exhaustive comparative records from the common sense in step with the reason) are completed, one will find an affirmation has crystalized. "What the mind keeps before it will depend largely on what it left behind." This affirmation which has been distilled by the boiling away of similarities has now condensed before the reason. It must now become an object of study and be broken down. This is the first vintage. *This is an induction.* Here, *a new utilitarian object has been anticipated,* a group of simple natures designed into a given nature.

The challenge here is to proceed in the natural sciences in such a way as not to appear to be doing anything more than improving the human state of affairs for one's nation. Knowledge must be seen as power for the state in order that the state not be weakened by idle, reflective men building mountains of words in magnificent castles. A state should not be populated by the idle, indigent dreamer who roams the roadsides of the state and robs and steals for his bread. A state of butterflies and caterpillars is a weak and puny society which will be defeated and occupied by some powerful enemy. The state that will be powerful and that will be a god to other states will be the state made up of the ants and the spiders working inductively from efficient causes. Galileo's glasses are not useful to the state, because he points them at the moon.

We need not be afraid of high numbers or minute fractions as long as they are explanatory of useful works at hand. Theology depends upon the will of man. Science depends upon the power of man. Power is subordinate to will. The good originates in God. Men must have tenderness and hope or else they will acutely feel their misery. The kingdom of God does not come with observation (Daniel); the divine works precede any human knowledge of the same. The true philosopher will learn from the memory of the spider and the industry of the ant. Natural philosophy should be pure and unmixed. It has been corrupted by the theology of Plato and the logic of Aristotle, and by mathematics. Vain apprehension is a problem. The natural philosopher should be like Alexander, and have none of the vain apprehension that comes with hearsay. In this way, what may be accounted as great will not seem great merely because rumor has it so. Scraps of gossip must not be taken as lawful information. This is the cause of much problem in politics. In politics, lawful information comes through state channels and not by gossip. This is the way it should be in natural philosophy. Legitimate interpretation demands that the scientist not decide beyond what the experiment allows.

Bacon avoids taking the step that Bruno took. Bruno defended the true *and* the good, as the useful. For Bacon, the true was the useful, *from* the natural sciences and *for* the state. This work of man was true insofar as it was harmonized with the fullest existential welfare possible for the state. The "good" could be given to faith if the scientist could keep the "true": the scientist's "true" should conform to the "good" of the official ideology on faith.

Bacon's remarks in Book I and II of the *Novum Organum* emphasize his view that men accomplish very little without orderly, systematic procedure. Trial and error that is tied to the human idols has produced only a few simple insights into natural law. And again, trial and error, tied to the human idols, has appropriated these few insights in a wasteful and non-productive manner. Bacon remonstrated that the scholars of his day were operating with blind, physical trial and error and had no ability to proceed along a middle path. This middle path would combine the common senses and the eager hands with pre-planned, reasoned observations upon descriptive, methodologically ordered data.

These writings call for the scientist as a "whole man", rather than a raw empiric or a soaring rationalist. This "whole man" is the scientist who sets aside conventional feelings and habit in order to give way to full observation. However, he does this with deliberate awareness of a premeditated commitment to demonstrative design which is committed to utility of an impersonal racial nature. The commitment here is to *social utility,* to the existential nation of men in the Philonic tradition. Bacon repeats Philo's concern that it would be a shame if the terrestrial globe was opened wide but the intellectual globe of man remained closed. Politics, or domestic housekeeping and philanthropia in the most reasonable way, could put England in the leadership role—as Bacon would say, "acting as god to man".

For Bacon, imitation of nature and corrected anticipation of nature coincided in legitimate interpretation of nature. Interpretation of nature entailed lawful attention to the precedence of the human. With his eye on human welfare, the scientist used natural history which was recorded human experience documented systematically to yield physical observations. These findings must be compared, with a view to the possibility that the evidence on hand may go beyond the goal by virtue of *the times*. If so, only the useful findings should be further pursued at that time.

Natural history in the past (recorded) and on-going nature study (recorded) provides the opportunity for *long-term preparation* of *the times* for innovations. The law of rulers proceeds unevenly, and the ways and means of collecting data will vary with the nature of the world. The nature of the world will eventually improve, due to the intellectual powers of men and the good will of faith which men have.

The state of society is analogous to the state of nature. It has the dual aspect of scientific curiosity and faithful piety. The existential amelioration of these two forces is prudence, which is the existential good. The prudent act, the prudent writing, is socialized reason that has the good of state foremost in view.

> But this is what will indeed dignify and exalt knowledge, if contemplation and action may be more nearly and straitly conjoined and united together than they have been; a conjunction like unto that of the two highest planets, Saturn, the planet of rest and contemplation, and Jupiter, the planet of civil society and action. (*A.L.*, I, v, 11)

(The material quoted from Bacon in this chapter is from the *Novum Organum,* reading for the most part with Fulton H. Anderson. The same points are often repeated in the *Advancement of Learning.*)

4.

COPERNICUS AND BACON'S SOCIALIZED SCIENCE

I T IS MY PRESENT POSITION that Bacon was not anti-Copernican (see Appendix A for references to Bacon's writings on this point). If Bacon had been anti-Copernican, he would have been able to expound such a position with safety. Bacon did reject Aristotle on many points, and says so. But when he mentions Copernicus—although he sometimes adds parenthetically that "this is not allowed"—his actual criticism of Copernicus turns out to be the Brunian complaint that "pure" mathematics could be a pitfall when applied to astronomy. Bruno constantly warns about forcing "pure" mathematical forms upon nature and obliterating natural facts; the mathematicians sometimes neglected to check their artistic webs for logical simplicity or to check them against plain experience. Bacon agreed that the mathematical furniture, if taken as superceding the missing phenomena, could be as much of a hardship for the progress of science as the churchman's celestially based religious entities.

Bacon criticizes Galileo's telescope in one place, saying it did not add to human welfare. But in another place, he praises it and gives mundane uses for it. This parallels his later desire to have his works read in Rome, where Galileo had friends and influence. As Tobie Matthew became close friends with Bellarmine, Bacon undoubtedly wanted to integrate into the continental scientific community. He says that he desired these contacts.

Bacon explains the old and the new astronomies as best he can. He remains non-committal. In one place he says, "This is pretty talk"; he is discussing the theory that "perpetual rotation" belongs

38

to the heavenly bodies and that "rest" belongs to the earth, and the theory that "heavy" bodies move downward to earth and "light" bodies move upward to the circumference of the heavens. Bacon's sarcasm here is the same as Bruno had published many years before. Bacon entertains Bruno's position that the air and waters surrounding the earth travel with the earth. At the crucial point, however, Bacon always publishes a statement which is either reasonably conservative or else ambiguous enough to protect him.

In the *Advancement of Learning,* Bacon wrote that he preferred to write what could be "believed" rather than to write what was to be merely "examined". In other places, Bacon frankly states that the reconstruction of learning demands that the understanding must be dilated to receive the facts of nature because the facts of nature could not be shrunk to fit the naïve understanding. This again sounds like Bruno and the other philosophers of nature of his period.

Bacon publishes in such a way that one cannot avoid understanding that he holds the planets and stars to be made of the same physical elements as the physical bodies on earth. "It is the perfect law of inquiry of truth that nothing be in the globe of matter, which should not be likewise in the globe of crystal or form; that is, that there be not anything in being and action, which should not be drawn and collected into contemplation and doctrine." (Form for Bacon was natural law.) Then he quickly adds that, of course, this science of truth is admittedly "inferior work". He states that a man must not abandon his fortune (even though his fortune is not an end worthy of his being) because fortune is an organ of virtue. Bacon points out with no value judgment that "many times men do abandon their fortune willingly for better respects."

Bacon refers to the study of heavenly bodies as being of a relatively "secret" nature. "Secret" is later explained as difficult to know or unfit to utter. He constantly tells us that method in science must not push for confrontation with "the times". Bacon published that:

> Not for any exact truth that can be expected in those theories; for
> as the same phenomena in astronomy are satisfied by the received

astronomy of the diurnal motion, and the proper motions of the planets, with their eccentrics and epicycles, and likewise by the theory of Copernicus, who supposed the earth to move, and the calculations are indifferently agreeable to both, so the ordinary face and view of experience is many times satisfied by several theories and philosophies; whereas to find the real truth requireth another manner of severity and attention. (*A.L.*, II, viii, 5)

If Bacon had been anti-Copernican, he would not have published this *at that time*. It was dangerous talk. I have come to the conclusion that Bacon probably was removed from office and his works confiscated because of his publishings in 1620. Bacon was indeed a shrewd merchant of ideas, whose long, hard, practical, and reflective labors did much to disseminate the most advanced ideas of his period. He did much to keep the work of Cusa, da Vinci, Copernicus, Bruno, Galileo, Telesio and others in useful flourish. Each man must be allowed to contribute in his own style. The Lord Chancellor and learned governor, Francis Bacon, served us well. We must not forget that Bacon reminded us what arts and sciences should be like. His voice is timely:

> Again, in the customs and institutions of schools, academies, colleges, and similar bodies destined for the abode of learned men and the cultivation of learning, everything is found adverse to the progress of science. For the lectures and exercises there are so ordered that to think or speculate on anything out of the common way can hardly occur to any man. And if one or two have the boldness to use any liberty of judgment, they must undertake the task all by themselves; they can have no advantage from the company of others. And if they can endure this also, they will find their industry and largeness of mind no slight hindrance to their fortune. For the studies of men in these places are confined and as it were imprisoned in the writings of certain authors, from whom if any man dissent he is straightway arraigned as a turbulent person and an innovator. But surely there is a great distinction between matters of state and the arts; for the danger from new motion and from new light is not the same. In matters of state a change even for the better is distrusted, because it unsettles what is established; these things resting on authority, consent, fame and opinion, not on demonstration. But arts and sciences should be like mines, where the noise of new works and further advances is heard on every side. But though the matter be so according to right reason, it is not so acted on in practice; and the points above mentioned in the administration and government of learning put a severe restraint upon the advancement of the sciences. (*N.O.*, I, xc)

Chapter Two

METHOD OF TRADITION RE-FORMED

1. Regulated Observation
2. Corrected Anticipation
3. Legitimate Interpretation

1.

REGULATED OBSERVATION

THE METHOD OF TRADITION is an existing social system of human power. This method of tradition reflects the dynamic relationship between human power and divine (natural) power upon which it has been based. "There is a kind of contract of error between the deliverer and the receiver" in the method of tradition. "For he that delivereth knowledge, desireth to deliver it in such form as may best be believed and not as best may be examined." (*A.L.*, II, xviii, 3)

Bruno had written, in *La Cena* (p. 123):

> To speak with the words of the truth where this is not appropriate is to want the vulgar and foolish multitudes, from whom one desires certain practices, to have the particular understanding in question; it would be like wanting to give eyes to the hands, which nature has not made to see but to physically manipulate, while giving consent to the sight. (The reader should also see *La Cena*, pp. 121, 122 and 124, in Gentile, or pp. 129-131 in Paterson, *The Infinite Worlds of Giordano Bruno*.)

If a scientific method for good human life is to grow and flourish, it must be secured not through glorifying one author or thinker. Men looking for vainglory do not serve scientific method. They are serving themselves. If one would desire merely blossoms, he may snip them off and wave them around or keep huge displays of blossoms around him. But they all soon wilt, and more and more must be garnered only to wilt. Nothing endures in this way.

However, if a man would transplant human power from one age into another, he must take up the roots. He must carefully transplant these roots where they can grow. He must be sure that everybody can see the little green shoots of early utility. Everyone must be called upon to help in his own way to nourish the little growth. Then, no one will fear the blossom which he himself

43

nourished. Here we see Bruno's "We look only for the fruit of the trees which we ourselves plant." Bacon writes that if the method of tradition is properly administered, "No man knoweth how he come by the knowledge which he obtaineth." Yet, some men will discern the sources of traditional knowledge, and they will "descend unto the foundations of their knowledge" and, finding the roots, will graft onto them interpretations from legitimate natural science. This grafting process should be imperceptible to the uninitiated. The technicians will protect these early growths, as they understand their utility and they are cultivators of knowledge. They have corrected anticipations.

For Bacon, no one person invented any ideas. Knowledge from men belongs to the human species. Therefore, men should look to the advancement of the human species in Time and not to the glorification of one man in any one time. Bacon would reject the provincial biographical history of physics and philosophy and the other sciences. However, during his times, he needed to tie his scientific truth to the glorification of the King of the new "Great Brittany". Like Bruno, Bacon had his reflective eye on the Kingdom of Men. Bacon understood that Time would level all monarchs eventually. Had not the Scriptures taught that the meek would inherit the earth?

Learned Governors worked prudently to insure the transplantation of sound judgment about experience into the next age. Bacon would have told Bruno (and perhaps he did) to feign conformity to *protect the work*. Since Bruno did not do so, Bacon tried to do it (*A.L.*, II, xvii, 1-5).

The method of tradition which was one aspect of human duty recognized the need for "placita juris" (willing assent or contract). This was aimed at civil utility and peace for the advancement of human welfare on earth. In duty to his own fortune (*A.L.*, II, xxiii, 161) a man should retain some suspension of belief but not so as to cause his own demise. The method of tradition is the coincident of the method of delivery (cultivation) of knowledge and of the method of invention (the interpretation of nature). Controversy in Bacon's times had caused "little inquiry" to go forward. The same problem held for civil business. The proper administration of philanthropia (justice for men on earth) and the proper administration for advancement of human learning were inexorably tied together, Bacon taught.

Judgment comes before delivery and judgment comes before invention. A system must be found which contains the *rules* for *judgment* (*A.L.*, II, xiii, 2). These rules should not only look to the *use* of knowledge. They should also look to the *advancement* of knowledge. One man cannot do it all in his lifetime. A tradition should be provided so that the torch of knowledge can be passed from one age to another. This entails a formal, administrative, documented structure for human scientific method which could endure through times. There should also be a diversity and plurality (tied to the utility of any one time) which would help insure that works would not be burned.

Systems of human intelligence should be concentric with the wheel of Time. Time has a dialectical nature, it goes backward and forward. The method of tradition should be like that. Established rules of judgment for the method of tradition are needed, to be sure that the method follows both use and advancement of knowledge.

Francis Bacon was born in the late sixteenth century and grew up in the monarchical context, imbedded in the royal family. From his earliest years, he was conditioned to the positive theory of knowledge about nature. His conditioning also fostered a ferociously competitive attitude toward worldly power, as England wavered unsteadily on her infant feet as a nation. Bacon was twenty-seven when the Spanish armada sank and England found herself catapulted into an international mystique about English power. It was up to England to hold that image—playing France against Spain—by dangling the friendship of the queen of the seas before each of them.

Francis Bacon cut his teeth on this kind of international diplomacy. Knowledge about how to gain wealth from the breast of nature insured England's safety. Knowledge about how to gain support from the breast of the monarch guaranteed Bacon's safety. *Systematic pursuit* was the only way in which men could achieve prudent power. For Bacon, nature had to be grasped through the visible physical forms and their operations, which, when sorely tried, would yield their contrary, latent structural connections.

This understanding of the latent law of a physical thing applied also to human persons. The monarch, like nature as a whole, remained always inscrutable, in part. The monarchy, because it was made of individuals of lesser natures that could be made transparent, was not able to evade analysis.

The nationalizing of scientific reason brought with it some problems for Bacon. This nationalizing process brought into existence a whole power structure for distribution and consumption of the goods of technology. There were the merchants, the lawyers, and the capitalists who emerged upon the scene because of talent as opposed to noble descent. The problem of monopolies and patents is the one which eventually broke the back of the monarch. The release of the scientific community from the control of the royal yoke was also accomplished through the emergence of this powerful middle class. This money class ultimately replaced the monarch as the absolute and became the controllers of the scientist and the technology.

When one removes the Monarch and removes the Scriptures as the two absolutes, this leaves polity to be expressed in only one way, through the one other absolute left, and that is Nature, Nature as exploited by a powerful money class composed of capitalists.

Scientific method as Bacon saw it meant control of the only absolute power left to scholars. And in his times, so frantically nationalistic, this meant English power. This line of reasoning led straight to the imperialism of the seventeenth, eighteenth, and nineteenth centuries, except that the royal driver had been replaced by the capitalist and the scientist. Therefore, in a sense, the nationalization of the scientific endeavor has culminated in the problems of the full-blooming twentieth century technocracy. Bacon correctly saw that one must invoke a rationalized absolute sacred myth (as did Plato) in order to explain (to the mass of men) the sacrifices involved; for the "many" lived to serve the technocratic absolute of profit. In technology, the capitalist and the scholars joined hands for nation.

Actually, Bacon was a political engineer, and he called his effort *philanthropia.* Bacon was a practical man of state. The duality of logical and physical was useful to him only to a restricted point. He wanted and needed immediate results of practical power. All of his long-term goals were tied to the survival of England as a nation. This meant that England should develop her own resources and the resources of all others in such a way as to insure her survival as a world power. How to accomplish this was Bacon's quest. The general logic of supreme nation was the latent form he sought as dormant behind the physical power of industrial science. In his role as pragmatic man of state, Bacon's use of Machiavellian reflection was marked. And yet, Bacon needed to couch all of this in the mood of good Christian morality. For him, Christian morality was the emblematic device for social control. Therefore, philanthropia had to be the apparent goal, not raw power. Bacon's definition of man as raw natural process if not defined according to the Christian sanction, mandated that individual men could only work out their rational destiny through the role of subject in a Christian state. In this way, a man could be realized, as he pursued his royal prerogatives (physical, emotional needs) through the royal prerogatives (physical, emotional needs) of the body congregate. The need of a rational society, through a planned ideology, supporting a planned technology for the individual good as it coincided with the congregate good, marks Bacon's philanthropia as a possible forerunner of Marx.

In Bruno, the Scriptures are the reservoir of useful metaphors, parables, similes, and examples that teach goodness. These symbolic devices are good in Bruno insofar as they reflect the natural, poignant struggle of men to realize the human good on earth. In Bacon, the Scriptures are a source of Revelation for the English monarch and his bishops. Bacon does insist that Revelation will not violate reason. But there is this difference between Bruno and Bacon regarding the ground for induction in the social sciences.

In Bruno, the logic of the syllogistic was not good for the natural sciences, because it did not follow *from* common sense observations (purged of fantastic habits). However, in Bruno, deduction was useful in testing inductive generalizations in the natural sciences. Moral theory for Bruno could take no liberties with induction. Moral theory that was expressed in metaphors and parables stood before reason *as* metaphors and parables. These were precious devices only insofar as they aided reason. In Bacon, moral theory could and did take liberties with inductions. Revelations could serve as the source of a religious syllogism. In Bacon, Deism could proceed dogmatically from the English version of the Scriptures. Bacon did not allow this irrational ground in the natural sciences. He was afraid of ultimate axioms there, and he said that the time was not ripe for ultimate axioms in natural science. In Bacon and Bruno, the social science, which is a tradition founded on natural law, cannot be understood apart from the natural science, which is also founded upon natural law. Man is taken as raw, logical power, and again as a socialized, conditioned power.

Bacon's sombre acceptance of the necessity for a nationalized science ("knowledge is power") marks *his own* Platonic synthesis. It was his solution to correct Machiavellian power and the superstition of Rome. For Bacon, these contraries would be coincidental in a humanistic polity. Baconian polity called for one nation, ruled by a learned-governor whose *reflective politics* provided a rational ideology for the power of the nation. In it the will bends the intellect and the intellect bends the reason, for domestic peace and for a social ideology. Particulars (subjects) are like an army, and the intellect (monarch) needs to know their strategy. The intellect (monarch) needs to hand this strategy over to the reason in order that critical men (royal administrators) could marshall a reasonable army (social executives). Decision is made on the basis of physical laws of human experience. Social physical argument is based on both inductive and deductive models, which are based on middle social axioms. These middle axioms are scales of justice whose weights remain in balance only if inductions and deductions are trimmed to match each other. This means that for the philosophers of natural *society,* reflective insight was no problem, as it was tested against bare physical law or social facts. For Bacon, reflective insight was incapable of forming middle axioms, if not from re-formed sensation in natural science. And social theory, *through Bacon,* demanded that *the middle axiom based upon intellectual intuition was legitimate* as long as the intellect had not been detached from the Scriptures for social theory. Here, the Scriptures supplanted Nature.

Bacon's concern was with good cause. Social control belonged to theological dogma. This entailed the excising of the intellect from its sensory matrix in the case of moral theory. For Bacon, moral theory could descend from supernatural models to meaningful moral middle axioms through theological Revelation supervised by the Vicar, the King. Morally, one needs the logical path of descent from faith's *remote* axioms. Morally, there are *not to be two paths* going in different directions, one from the middle axiom to the ultimate axiom, one from the ultimate axiom to the middle axiom. For Bacon, there *is to be* a two-lane highway supporting two-way traffic *for the natural sciences,* but the highway of morality is to have one lane, moving from top to bottom. This will facilitate domestic peace. First comes national unity; then comes implementation of natural science advanced through the domestic law and order. Progress is accomplished through the social submission of the subjects and through their obedience to the faithful Christian revelation, as understood and practiced by Christ's vicar on earth, the monarch.

Science was *useful* science. When Francis Bacon held that policy "è gemino" (Abbott, p. 189), he indicated that the metaphysical insight of his period pertaining to "the coincidence of contraries" represented the structure of both the state of nature and the state of human community. The absolute "nature" was to have been understood in terms of its visible forms and its latent configurations and its latent process. This means the tracing out of the latent forms by putting the visible forms through complete physical manipulations and trials, in order to wrench from them the latent formula of their physical operations. The absolute known as "the State" was to be understood in terms of its visible forms, the monarchy, and its latent form, the monarch. This means the tracing out of the power-pattern of the latent form by using physical manipulation and physical trial of the visible signs in order to *wrench* from the monarchy the *latent formula* of the hidden operation of the masses.

Once we grasped the logic of the latent process and latent configuration, we could then appropriate these formulae to our own uses. Applying them to the task of *human service,* as opposed to the task of blind cosmic cycle, in order to socialize science, Bacon saw that one would have to release social science from the grip of superstition. Moral values should not impede the proper exercise of free physical manipulation of all natural phenomena. Moral values must therefore be provided out of an entirely different frame of reference, having nothing to do with the search for the latent process or configuration behind non-human nature. Moral values, then, would be drawn up from the Holy Scriptures and have nothing at all to do with judging the work of science or technology.

Bacon recognized three realms of human reality. One, the moral realm; secondly, the political realm; thirdly, the science of nature. The moral realm was monistic and dogmatic. It was to remain in service to the political realm. The political realm was the more fundamental. It was didactic, and it was understandable in terms of two absolutes; one was nature, and the other was the monarchy. The theme of *naturans-naturata*—the theme of the one and the many—was exercised here. These two arms of polity, nature and monarchy, could be understood from either aspect. Nature had dual aspects and so did monarchy.

Philanthropic power renewed itself through its practical fruits for Bacon. When Bacon spoke of Machiavelli, he said that Machiavelli was correct in understanding that the ruler should work with people in a very practical way by manipulating them on the basis of an understanding of their frailties and vulnerabilities and a realistic recognition of their strengths. But he adds that Machiavelli did not have his eye upon the good life that was possible for man, but rather used the method with a view to sustaining the status quo. For Bacon, men could come to desire a common good and be conditioned to a minimal obedience through common reasonable moral teachings, as in the Philonic tradition.

One would proceed in the manipulation of men exactly as one would proceed in the manipulation of all nature. Men should be studied and their needs and powers completely understood. Then these needs should be met, and their powers should be used. Strict and corrective external procedures were to be used to command morality, just as strict external procedure should be used to command other kinds of nature for knowledge, in order that it too should serve the human scene with power. In the case of morality, Bacon used the Scriptures as this axiomatic device to provide the moral blueprint for the correction of human frailty. During his career Bacon developed many lasting relationships with individuals of different faiths from his own. For a subject in England, however, Bacon would hold that the monarchical requirement to practice English morality would entail an oath of allegiance to the English Bible.

He also saw the necessity for the role of the clergy as the keepers of the faith among the people, through the monarch's grace. Heresy in religion could be, for Bacon, a dangerous and fruitless posture for a member of any society to be allowed to practice. This would be nature unharnessed. However, one is reminded of Bacon's position that in order to be commanded, nature must first be obeyed. Unlike Hobbes, Bacon neglected to provide for the human specimen of nature his inherent right to be outraged by a forced oath of allegiance in the event that he could not base his moral principles upon the Scripture's story of the fall of ordinary men.

Bacon had lived through the persecution of many people in England and on the Continent because of their failure to meet the social requirement of adherence to their society's use of the concept of a supernatural God. Bacon spent many hours in service to the throne actually participating in their downfall and torture. The case of Edmond Peacham, a clergyman charged with treason as the author of an unpublished treatise justifying rebellion against oppression, is one such example. And Bacon had lived through the burning of Bruno, whom he undoubtedly knew and probably had met both in France and in England. He was also aware of Galileo's problem in 1616.

Cardinal Bellarmine, who prosecuted both Bruno and Galileo and later converted Bacon's best friend (Tobie Matthew) to Romanism (see letter in Appendix B), was a very powerful man on the Continent, and Bacon wanted free correspondence abroad. Bacon's old friend and personal censor, Andrews, a clergyman, was engaged in attempting to refute a Jesuit publication which libeled Elizabeth. All of this was important to Bacon, because he was kept poignantly aware of the extent to which conflicts about religious faith seemed to be a main impediment to human progress. He seems always to have maintained the attitude that, apart from minimal loyalty oaths, most people should be left alone to practice their English Faith in their own way. He seemed to feel that each nation had the right to nationalize its religious practices for the glorification of God and its monarch.

However, he criticized the practices of Rome as being unduly laden with superstitious ritual, and in a letter to Tobie went so far as to suggest that superstition about these matters was worse than not believing in any of it. This writer holds that because of the *very huge* amount of manuscripts and writings which Bacon had amassed from all over England and the Continent and the East and the New Lands (in order to organize and classify and compile enough data that the search for some fruitful middle axioms or ideas for experiments could be facilitated), he had come to realize that what faith a man had in religious matters or what nation he was at home in made little difference in the value of his ideas as far as technology was concerned. All of these ideas and practices that Bacon accumulated seemed to drive him with an impatience to set aside the issues that seemed not relevant to the command of inanimate physical nature, and to proceed quickly to the task of producing demonstrable power over inanimate natural resources in order to lift the condition of men in this world. Bacon held that the behavior of men would be more likely to improve in due course, if his existential conditions improved.

England, the nation, was ruled over by a monarch of royal blood who had unalterable prerogatives. This theory of the royal prerogatives was carried over by Bacon into a theory of technological research. Nature was analogous to the monarch. She would not and could not bend. If one would command her (get her attention, influence her to move in a prescribed way), one must obey her first. In all of Bacon's letters to Essex, this admonition in regard to Elizabeth is repeated. Bacon practiced this principle of conduct with the throne very carefully, most of the time.

With the monarchical process of nature, also, one needed to recognize the royal prerogatives. This was his complaint with the rationalists, who, he felt, had lost their petition with nature because they had not paused to observe her long enough to find out exactly where she was vulnerable to manipulation or communication. He criticizes Aristotle very smartly on this point. It would be as if these men reflected upon an audience with the majesty of nature and then, without the actual experience, would proceed to record it as if in fact it had taken place. Bacon, on the other hand,

knowing the capricious *and* universally oriented aim of the royal
tasks, knew well that any particular petition must be delivered
with painstaking precision and accuracy, and repeated hundreds
of times and revised, to suit the *mood* of any majestic. He also
knew well that the laws which drove the majestic were hardly
aimed toward the survival of the kingdom at large at all times.

From his very early days in the Commons, Bacon was well
aware that fools may speak where wiser men have learned to hold
their tongues. Elizabeth had for years refused even to receive him
because he publicly criticized her request for taxes from the common. In a monarchy, to a man who wanted to be at England's
helm, this was a devastating loss to his career. In perfect accord
with this lesson and with all he observed further in the behavior
of human natures, Bacon sharply criticized men who attempted to
walk up to the majestic nature and force her through impulsive
pushings to yield her laws of operation. These empirics, Bacon
thought, were too hasty, and would meet only rebuff.

Francis Bacon has been traditionally presented as a philosopher,
as a scientist, as a literary giant, as a genius of universal nature,
and as a follower of Machiavelli in the applied sense. None of
these treatments of the man grasp the essential *unity* of his life
and the great endurance and stamina that his life exemplifies.
When one examines carefully just how Bacon functioned, one finds
that the doggedness and patience and extreme tenacity that he demonstrated in seeking the ear and the eye of the throne must either
point to an extreme case of megalomania or else to some deep
inner conviction that could be understood as nationally oriented
or aimed. The more closely one examines the hours and days that
Bacon spent in service to Elizabeth and James in an attempt to
pull them out of trouble or to provide a guidance to them in times
of hard domestic crisis, the more one recognizes that Bacon had
no other life but the life of England, and no greater concern than
England's welfare and survival. Although Bacon lived lavishly
and with an entourage of over two hundred in a quasi-court of his
own at the Inn, at York, at Gorhambury, and at Twickham, none
of this splendor was for Bacon the man. There was only England
and the need to be kept constantly informed of the court, of the
Continent, of Ireland, of Scotland, and of all the writings and re-

searches going on in England and on the Continent. There were
the New Lands and the expeditions to keep track of, in terms of
England and her international rivals. There was the role of barrister for the crown in the Commons, and later the actual concrete
duties of the Solicitor General and Attorney General and finally
Lord Chancellor.

Bacon lived and behaved as a prince. This fact should not be
ignored or denied. He received all that he ever got by royal favor
because he demanded it, and threatened and cajoled and per-
sistently insisted on it. Bacon worked the clock around for the
monarchs and suffered great and persistent defeats, but never became defeated by this humiliation. Bacon was repeatedly humili-
ated before the entire populace by the throne, but, always un-
daunted in his persistent way, would accept the insult and doggedly
await the chance to renew his petition and assistance to the throne.
Actually, as one studies the functioning of Bacon, one sees clearly
that Bacon methodically wore the monarchs down, with both the
patience of a Job and the persistent determinations of a king to save
his land. Nowhere in all of the record is there any evidence that
Bacon took anything at all for himself as an individual. All of
the funds he received were spent directly on his own court of men,
to meet the expenses of his work.

Bacon saw readily that knowledge of the mastery of every single
natural resource he could get his hands on was needed in order
that it be converted into English power. From all sides England was
under dire threat of destruction. The authority of Rome had not
accepted the autonomy of the English nation, and looked upon
her as an errant child to be forced back into the fold. No effort
was ignored by Spain to effect the return of England to the authority of Rome. Ireland and Scotland were constantly demanding
their freedom from England, and there were constant military
expeditions into these places by England, who could not afford to
have them turn hostile to her as independents. Spain was constantly
called by the Irish to assist their cause, and landing on Irish soil
to fight the English. In England itself, the situation remained grave
in all of Bacon's years, due to internal treasonable sects who never
had accepted the break with Rome. There were also other radical
religious groups, such as the Calvinists, who did not believe that

the break with the old religion was severe enough, and maintained that a complete reform was in order. The espionage by Spain and Rome right in the English court was very active and persistent. In Bacon's time several attempts made on Elizabeth's life involved persons who had had the trust of the court. All of these problems found Francis Bacon on the front line of action, because he was expected to be there and because he wanted to be there. Any attempt to present Bacon as a man of leisure who languished over a plush library reading and studying for months at a time is not one which follows the facts.

Actually Bacon frantically gathered all the books and writings he could. He had a large number of men scribes writing and rewriting and reading to him as much of the time as he had to spare for it. His personal confidant and secretary, Rawley, states that Bacon was not at all careful about the manner in which he used the work of other authors. Most of the later writers on Bacon also acknowledge this fact. But it would be crude and completely without insight to oversimplify the case by saying that Bacon was dishonest in this way. It would be to apply our standards to a time that was not at all ready for a rigorous exercise of proper protocol regarding references.

Bacon's published works all seem to be compilations from the many works that he had collected in order that he might weave them together to form a new English *catechism of knowledge* for the education of Englishmen. Upon this new organization of knowledge Bacon wanted to build scientific theory that would be fruitful in terms of industrial results. It should be understood that Bacon compiled and amassed a huge amount of writings from all over—in correspondence, and by courier, and by purchase—in order to build the best possible library in all of the world, one that would hold all the most fertile ideas in the world for producing material things for the power of England at home and abroad. When Bacon died, a lot of material that was left behind was published as his, but it does not follow that it was written by Bacon.

After James became king and spent considerable time in Scotland on extended holidays, during which he took the court with him, Bacon took over the reins and received ambassadors and scholars from all over the world at Whitehall. Bacon had seen

Europe as a young man and wanted to have in England a court as enriched and as informed as were those in France and Italy. His brother Anthony had done intelligence work from the Continent for over sixteen years, and there was not very much that had gone on in those places that Bacon had not heard about. During this time, Parliament began to manifest its fight to test the king's royal prerogative. James could not handle the Parliament. It was Bacon, a former member of the Commons himself, with twenty-five years' experience behind him in practical political compromise between the throne and the new middle class, who forestalled temporarily the chaos that climaxed in the reign of Charles I, who was beheaded by the Parliament. The end of royal prerogative began with the unseating of Bacon as Lord Chancellor, and leadership for industrial giantism took the path of personal profit and power, as against the path of a systematized and orderly development of natural resources according to the planned society of a Lord Chancellor.

One leaves the works and writings of Bacon with a sombre and remarkable pessimism regarding the future of societal man. The altruism that Bacon practices toward the common person is a mechanical and contrived apparatus which boils down to a means of applying a procedural yoke to a half-beast in order to insure the promise of a planned societal strategy of national survival. Man does not develop from the inside out in dynamic interplay with rich personal experience, as in the philosophers of nature on the Continent at this time; rather, man develops as a subject through the adjustment to the cultural yoke of a designed technological power-thrust by the politically versed and royally endowed. In truth, human life at its best seems to be not much different from that which Machiavelli paints, even though Bacon feels that his own system points to the good life, as opposed to the system of Machiavellian man, which merely aims toward perpetuation of power.

If the Baconian horizons seem to be mere mirages, one needs to ask why they appear in this way. The answer comes slowly and painfully. It appears that the analysts who sit in twentieth century studies invoke a theory of altruism hardly appropriate to Elizabethan England. Moving in those times and carefully extracting demonstrable bits of the societal fabric from that period, one is enabled to correct the methodological distort. For Bacon there was only one survival at stake. It was the survival of England. It would be several hundred years before the nations on the Continent made such a daring pitch for political autonomy based on industrial know-how. Bacon saw the only way to gain this as being industrial development through social order: a planned nation rich in a controlled technology and justified by a sacred moral dogma.

The acquisition of knowledge was for Bacon a way to insure political supremacy. Long before the Royal Society was founded, Bacon supported and operated his own laboratory of knowing and his own world library of manuscripts, attended by a veritable court of scribes and mechanics. When it was said that Bacon wrote philosophy like a Lord Chancellor, the statement was correct. In this truth, the writer sees no devaluation of Bacon's monumental contribution to the development of the industrial scientific nation that is based on the pragmatic command of all of that nation's natural resources, human or otherwise.

2.

CORRECTED ANTICIPATION

THE IMPLEMENTATION of scientific knowledge for the societal kingdom of man was another whole challenge; Bacon distinguished this from the discovering of or the acquiring of that knowledge of the kingdom of nature.

In Bacon's time, the only safe ideology to be used as the guide for integrating the societal kingdom and the kingdom of nature, was the Scriptures. Bacon was willing to appropriate the Scriptures to this use through the decisions of a committee of scientists who would determine what to hand over to the monarch. As an ideological instrument, the Scriptures could be used to control the use of scientific invention and technology. Therefore, the Scriptures must be preserved so they would mandate popular appreciation of English nation and English power.

There is not the originality in Bacon that some in the literature claim for him. Fischer, Farrington, and Anderson (see Bibliography at the end of this volume) deal with this. What we see in Bacon, as in the writings of his time, is the appreciation that human habits can be used and manipulated as any other natural power. Social control was a necessary activity. If one studies man one understands how and in what fashion men can be controlled. If one wants to control inanimate nature one proceeds in the same way. The trick lies in the *identification of resources* and the *implementation of these resources* through system. System for nation was imbedded in the interplay of moral and practical. Moral system for Bacon must take advantage of the Idols of the human nature and provide the ideology which would produce national loyalty and domestic peace. Practical system must *avoid* the Idols of the human nature and tear aside the social posture in order that the scientist can look fully upon the natural process in order to see what part of it can be wrested from the silent cosmos and be heralded as man-made art. Bacon quotes the Psalm "that the eyes of the handmaiden look perpetually to the hands of her mistress" (*Works*, V, p. 20). And he adds Cicero's insight that gestures unlock and open the doors of the mind (*Works*, V, p. 74). Bruno wrote in the *Eroici Furori* that the hunter must become his prey. Bacon repeats this point (*Works*, V, p. 24). Bacon writes that the vale discovers the hill as inferiors discover their superiors (*Works*, V, p. 15). Bacon writes that from a man's household the "winds inherit much" and the man's reputation dies (*Works*, V, pps. 41, 43, 47, 50, 63). This discussion is centered around the proverbs of Solomon. Bacon's commitment to practical cooperation with the king (nature) is paralleled by the same commitment to the king (nation). To be commanded, both monarchs must be obeyed. The master-servant interplay is important in both cases here. A good servant (handmaiden or scientist) was, for Bacon, one who was master of his charge because he knew so much about the nature of his charge that, as servant, he manipulated the situation for his own designs.

Francis Bacon was stripped of power in 1621, one year after his book the *Novum Organum* was published. Like Galileo, Bacon had misjudged his opponents' strength. In the book Bacon takes the royal prerogative and hands it over to nature. He also states that change and innovation is the only hope for human welfare. Although Bacon is careful to say that this does not apply in the case of civil government, one sees easily that the monarchy Bacon paints is one which must be reigned over by a benevolent despot, namely a learned governor. The myth of royal bloodline had caused England a great deal of harm. The War of the Roses and Henry VII's resolution to the problem satisfied Bacon. In the Philonic tradition, the fittest man for leadership would be the noble one. The learned governor was the royal man for Bacon, too, as he was high in the kingdom of nature (which undercut the kingdom of man, unless man respected nature's reality). To name a monarch by bloodline and not by natural prowess was for Bacon a costly thing to do. He said, "Nature to be commanded must be obeyed," and he meant it. The plan which is presented in the

Novum Organum and in the *Advancement* was a marked threat to James and his favorites. It was all Coke needed to mark Bacon as a danger to the throne.

There had never been a time when Bacon had not been a constant reminder to Burleigh that there were factions in the court waiting for the power. Anthony Bacon also resented the way in which those most able were held in the background and nondescript parasites with the cunning of foxes controlled the sympathies of the Monarch.

The *Novum Organum* is abruptly cut off. After study of Book II it is not difficult to reconstruct what might have followed in Book III if we could read it. Upon the death of Coke all of Coke's works and papers were seized and destroyed. It is my hypothesis that most of Bacon's *Novum Organum* was seized also (after the king or his agents had read it), and that Bacon was removed from public office because he was seen as a threat to the power of the throne. His enemy Coke may indeed have offered the judicial framework of the bribe, but this is hardly a credible charge as far as the customs of patronage in government are concerned. The real reason for the treatment of Bacon can be found in the flavor of the *Novum Organum* which clearly states that the monarchy, which is the analogue of nature, is a creation of people, and that to function well the monarchy must be constructed and planned rationally according to the experience of the human race, and not according to the irrational politics as they were in that day. Bacon held that to explicate the hidden forms or laws was the way to wrench power from nature and superimpose human intelligence upon it (he wrote a book on Henry VII, who took the throne by force). In this way man becomes creator of the existential world and could bend nature to his foresight and his designs. Exactly the same method holds for Nature and for Monarchs in Bacon—and he says so. He is careful, but he notes that the manner of choice of rulers in his day is unforgivably bad (*N.O.*, II, xlviii, and *A.L.*, I, ii, 1, 3, 7, 9, and II, xxiii, 49). The whole idea of *transferring* the royal prerogative from the throne to the physical nature in which men lived was the theme of the Italian philosophers of nature, and Bacon readily adopted it as long as he could divest it of any superstition that might remain in it. For Bacon, the Idols of the human species must be identified and put under control. They were tribal and could be *appropriated for matters of social control;* but in matters of natural science they must be set aside. In matters of natural science, the moral ideology of the Scriptures (used to further the Idols of the human nature) must be ignored. Disciplined scientists must be allowed to observe and to manipulate visible nature freely. Moving in the spirit of the Greek distinction between the visible and the invisible, Bacon distinguished between the visible nature of the world which must be understood to be cloaking its own invisible nature, and the invisible nature of the world which was the moral nature of the world and which also cloaked its essential laws in the Monarch.

The two must not be confused. If the spiritual or moral aspect of the world (which was peculiar to man) was to be explained in terms of the visible or physical aspects of the world, this would be mixing science with superstition. One should not confuse the matter with the opposite error, either. One should not try to explain the physical or natural sciences in terms of the moral or spiritual aspects of the world. This again would be mixing the scientific with the superstitious.

It should be remembered that Bacon lived at a time when he could have been arrested and jailed and executed upon a moment's notice if he threatened either the throne or the throne's religious teaching. This was a real and substantial concern for Bacon and he states as much. He even went further and sent all his work to Tobie Matthew, who had turned Catholic (in order that his work not be lost to the Catholics because they might violate the religious teachings). Tobie was to censure the work for him.

Here is the great problem in Bacon. He called for change in the natural sciences. Change and innovation were the two basic values he held that would free the natural sciences from alchemy and scholasticism. And yet, he states that these changes and innovations are *not* to bring forth social upheaval. What is necessary here is planned technology, planned research teams. There would be no limit in the pursuit of nature's secrets, but the power which resulted must be in the hands of the planners for the nation. Industrial science is a practical endeavor, and, as such, it should be integrated so as not to bring abortive changes in the social customs. One of the chief means for insuring domestic peace, Bacon thought, was imperialism. The lowliest Englishman must be head and shoulders above those he conquers, by virtue of the fact that he is an Englishman. In this way, the industrial power of the nation can be kept by the guardians of the nation, while the bulk of the populace is kept satisfied and is kept busy, producing the instruments which would conquer the lesser of the human species. Bacon taught that benevolent despots were the answer. In relation to the rest of the world, every Englishman was to become just that.

Human talent in Bacon's time was greedily consumed by the monarch upon his mere whim. Probably no greater example of this can be found than in the reign of Elizabeth. The huge amount of talent (both foreign and domestic) which gathered about her was astounding. Her ruthless employ of all they had to give was a monumental example of the state above all else. Taken in the context of the times, one sees easily that she had no alternative. The survival of England depended upon this huge exploitation of human talent at any cost.

Bacon was immersed in the death struggle that England waged for her own survival, and saw that this survival depended upon aggression in foreign policy. Bacon's view of the planned society is a direct result of the times in which he functioned. He saw the reign of Henry VII as a model: and it was in this reign that the throne became the repository for the country's wealth. In Bacon's own time, through Elizabeth I, the throne again became the repository where the wealth of the nation should be lodged alongside of the royal prerogatives of the guardian of that nation. The problems were that the middle class was growing too fast and that the natural sciences were taking a back seat to the geographical swellings.

Bacon's model for the academics of the natural sciences was not original; teams of scholars were at work on common problems in many courts. What Bacon did understand well was that the problems which were being worked on were hopelessly provincial in their scope. Bacon, the man noted for his fear of speculative philosophies, was not without speculative leanings here. Bacon wanted universal and very general areas of study set up. He appreciated that the nation which could fill the role of benevolent despot would be that nation which took all of nature to be its province. Bacon believed in the philosopher-king of Plato and was convinced that "might" was not the sword but the knowledge which other men needed. England was to have that knowledge and would fulfill the role of learned governor among the nations.

The average man for Bacon was a natural specimen that was expendable. Bacon was thus in perfect accord with the Christian teaching that God gave each man his station in this life as a trial to earn grace for the next life. Bacon as political engineer was convinced that the kingdom of nature and the kingdom of God were more or less parallel and that any imperfections in the parallelity were due to errors of judgment in the third kingdom, the kingdom of man. Bacon conducted himself always as if he were one of the elite of the three kingdoms.

Although Bacon held that might was knowledge, this does not mean that Bacon held to a good Samaritan policy for the affairs of men. Knowledge of a man should result in control of that man. There were no holds barred in maintaining one's advantage over that of his competitor in the society. Competition among the elite was understood. The simple people competed on their level and the two classes, noble and common, had to be kept in a critical balance by "noble" leadership.

In Bacon, to form axioms from experience, we proceed from sense to memory to reason. We must use induction, as the understanding must be guided and directed. We discover, we do not imagine. We need a natural history as a foundation. Bacon seemed to call for a text from which the inquiry of human curiosity could begin its labor. He called it a foundation of natural history. Bacon's natural history would be essentially different from the scholastic catechism, because it would be systematized questions and answers about the material and efficient causes of existential bodies.

Bacon saw the Book of Common Prayer as useful. The Scriptures were the counterpart to the Natural History, the "common book" of nature. How could one divide the Natural History from the Scriptures? By licensed revelation through politically controlled theology. Bacon quotes the Scriptures in his writings and his *Essays* even though he deplored the idea that cosmologies were often written in deference to the Scriptures. Inasmuch as knowledge in physics was to be tailored to the policy of the benevolent absolute rulers of the nation, and the nation was to be morally pivoted on the Christian Scriptures, it seems difficult in the end to account for Bacon's criticism.

The use of natural philosophy seems to be completely at the mercy of these Revelations from the theologian, although Bacon says that the scientist may or may not reveal all of his discoveries to a Monarch.

Bacon states that one should not try to understand him as an armchair philosopher who is neatly tucked away in a sumptuous study with quiet and time and money at his disposal. With candor, Bacon points to the fact that he is hopelessly bogged down with a very active role in the state and has to beg and fight for funds in order to keep his personal court satisfied.

It must be understood that Elizabeth expected her statesmen to pay for their own intelligence and supplies and personnel. The funds she awarded them would scarcely cover these expenses, and they were expected to supply additional funds for their work by receiving funds from patronage. It was a matter of survival for the state to raise the necessary monies to keep the protestant cause alive in western Europe. It was a matter of survival for the state to keep Spain out of Ireland and to keep France out of Scotland. This took a great deal of money.

The throne must also present a sumptuous court. One could not expect the Englanders to understand the power of the Tudor throne unless that throne presented face and brawn and power comparable to the courts of Spain, France, and Rome. The receptions held for foreign ambassadors must be able to intimidate them with the power image of the Queen and her people. Elizabeth could not afford to allow her nobles and her courtiers to accumulate private fortunes. They were expected to invest their money and holdings along with the throne as partners.

It is nonsense to describe the habit of patronage in Tudor England as bribery. Actually there was not so much pride in money for itself during this period. The money was only a means toward the end of preserving the corporate state. The courtier had to put it all right back into the expenses of his office. What really was the acme of satisfaction was the victory of a noble *name*. The businessman could cross from commoner to noble by virtue of his wealth. At this point he was given a noble name. In this way he became a member of the board of directors of the corporate state and would enter into direct business contracts with the throne for the making of profit from the sea and its trade. He would also provide arms and men for the military. In order to remain in good grace he must compete with the other noble names.

Bacon never had any money. He was not able to compete with the new breed of entrepreneur. He could not afford to buy into their stock companies nor could he command troops. He was never in the public eye as a great favorite. Rather, Bacon remained to the public and to most of the court as a shadowy power who was enigmatic and powerful but totally English. This latter trait was very important because there were many noble and courtly powers at this time in England who did not feel that the break with Rome was necessary. Bacon was not one of these.

Bacon spent millions of dollars and lived as a prince. The funds were obtained through loans and grants directly from the throne or through the lands granted him by the throne. The money was used to support his own minor court of men who were encyclopedists and intelligence agents. Knowledge *was* power for Bacon, and he made no distinction in his budget between the value of knowledge of natural sciences and the value of knowledge of the political intrigue in the domestic or foreign courts.

Probably the one trait Bacon had which set him apart from a great many of his peers was his impersonal ambition to sustain the re-formed use of human intelligence. The pirates and the businessmen had English loyalty tied to *personal* profit. Bacon did not. His loyalty to the English throne was born of a sense of destiny for the nation. Bacon saw a planned nation in England. He tried to write the blueprint for that planned nation. It would excel all other nations just because it was planned and not based upon maudlin superstition or fear. The people would conform because they would be comfortable and fairly content, and the monarch would be loved and revered because he would be informed and prudent and the most powerful monarch in the world. The influence of the middle books of Plato's *Republic* is quite apparent here. Yet Bacon thinks more in terms of a learned governor or a political engineer than in terms of a philosopher king, probably in spirited reaction to the high scholastic practices prevalent in the English universities of his time.

It is Bacon himself who emerges as the engineer for the planned state. The time was ripe, and England dared to make the pitch for existential autonomy based upon raw might and rationalization. Bacon understood there were two kinds of power. He did not contribute as a soldier or as a pirate. He saw his role as that of providing the political engineering which would guide the revolution from the age of superstition.

Religion, for Bacon, could be a means to serve the ends of an enlightened state. By no license would he assent to the enlightened state as a means to the ends of a religion. This is very crucial. Religion is an ideology which was to provide an explanation for the de facto re-formed state. For him, religion was a rationale. Man was different from the other species because he could be rational and he could design his state, even if part of his design was intentionally to remain ancient. The Scriptures were the history of the slow emergence of reason and insight which the human race had gleaned from social experience. Reflective men who had contemplated the human scene presented these Revelations which had been hard won. Bacon felt that they were useful.

During the years of his life, it would not have been possible for him to have discarded them. Atheism would mean death or exile, and Bacon was interested in serving England.

3.

LEGITIMATE INTERPRETATION

THE THEMES OF THE RENAISSANCE threw out the invisible man. As the practical arts forged ahead, men became aware of human power and its profits. The thorough exchange of culture due to massive changes in the naval arts exposed Western man to the ideologies of the forgotten past which were of material bias.

The speculative theocratic social dogmas could not control the advance in the practical and theoretical sciences, and the old world came to its demise. Now man would live in full and complete respect for the visible man who confronted him in the mirror. The visible man as God's finest achievement was challenged by the task of realizing his fullest exercise of human power. Literally, the visible man went into partnership with God.

As God created the first world, man would create the second world. This second world would be the kingdom of man, which would be the result of bringing human power to bear on the given world of nature. Converted nature, now the man-made image of ultimate power, could demonstrate man's appreciation of the God-given world. Man could do this by transforming it into the world of good men who led the good life.

The good life was no longer the life after death, to provide a salvation for the invisible man. The good life now was seen as the realization of the natural world through the re-construction of the natural sciences. *Politics was now joined to philosophy,* whereas, before, politics had been left to the religious impulse. Through conformity to a religious dogma, man had obeyed the ultimatum to save his soul and leave the physical world to the inspired leadership of the divine and royal leaders who would manage all human voyages through this valley of tears.

Western philosophy had been tied to the exoneration of the

theological dogma and had not been given the challenge of defining the good life in terms of its own activity and insights. Western philosophers had bent the intellect to prove the existence of the invisible man and the invisible God who controlled him.

Philosophy now became alive with the recalled Hebraic, Arabic, Greek and Roman philosophies of existential nature, which in turn hearkened back to the Eastern ideologies of far older cultures such as Babylonia and Egypt. Man looked into nature now and saw his own image. Man was at home in nature now and soon saw the way to build a new nature upon the naïve nature in order that the human race might live well and prosper. This was the finest salute to God possible. It entailed full use of the gift of life and nature rather than the abuse of it.

How would philosophy provide the plan for the societal heaven which should mirror the religious one? Where would reflection turn for its new values? There was a pluralism. Some philosophers remained within the Christian fold and for all practical purposes separated the existential man from his soul. Existential values would replace spiritual values in the practical sphere of everyday life, but the spiritual values would hold outside of the natural sciences.

In these cases natural sciences were cut off from the moral life. Two sets of operations were installed. Existential profit was a very high and legitimate value, but it was rationalized as being a reward from God because of special grace and blessedness. Therefore, the successful would support the religious dogma as a way of giving "hope and tenderness" (Bacon) to the lesser endowed.

Another group of philosophers became frankly agnostic. These thinkers taught that nothing could be known about Origin, God, or First Cause, and therefore man should pick up his life and make it worthy of his human powers. A humanized cosmos was the only sane cosmos and the fine arts demonstrated the pathos of the mystery that man must learn to live with. The best that could be done was to exercise a reverence toward each man and afford him the dignity of his species. In this way each man would become an end to be realized in his own natural right, as opposed to being a means of perpetuating a human valley of tears, ruled by tyrants.

Bacon emerged upon the scene thirty years after England had

undergone massive change in her value system. The autonomy of the English nation had been initiated, but was still very tenuous. Bacon was steeped in the new role of the contemplative man. He studied all the political scripts of these old traditions and was conditioned to the value that national autonomy could be accomplished only with full dedication to material profit and material power. There were no illusions in the royal court of Bacon's England as to how the autonomy of the nation could be won.

Bacon thought that, all through history, there had been two alternatives. Either one ruled, or he was ruled. If a man would rule he should rule well. This entailed wisdom, and wisdom entailed philosophy. If the non-philosophical man ruled, then the chances of his ruling well would not be as great because the man who turned (for wisdom) merely to the past would not be able to cope with the ever-changing present, or with the future.

Therefore, the political man must emerge in his own right. This man would make a careful and dedicated study of his pursuit, which would include "taking all of knowledge to be his province." Only in this way could he be prepared to rule with an eye on the future of mankind, and an eye on the present circumstances. The past would be studied as it served to illuminate the present or the future. The past history of mankind would be used as raw material in an inductive way to ascertain the latent law of the political pursuit. The art of rule would be patterned upon the natural sciences, for the art of rule *was* a natural science.

The rule of a knowledgeable and reflective bastard was to be preferred to the rule of a royal or ecclesiastical moron or an academic ass. The societal fabric that men would graft upon the given nature would be based on the laws of nature and not on the fantastic laws of superstition. Here we see a return to the Philonic tradition where the Scripture must be informative to the reason of men. The exegesis of the Scriptures would be undertaken by reflective man in order that no wisdom from the past be lost. The laws of past successful human experience should be understood and studied. They demonstrated man in his human dignity and in control of his exquisite powers for obtaining the fullest realization of his human potential. The reading of the Scriptures by the non-reflective man would also serve the society, because the Scriptures recorded much in the sort of allegory that facilitated rapid and complete grasp of much insight by any man with normal intelligence. The reflective man could assist in this interpretation of the Scriptures, as he seemed most fitted for this job; however, he could not violate the reasonable faculty of his people. There was no reason at all for his people to be forced to believe the unreasonable.

All of this had been taught by Philo Judaeus. Bacon was attempting to carve out the rules of good politics; so he followed this Philonic tradition that had been used through many centuries. Bacon lived at a time when this was not easy. He adapted his model to suit the readiness of his times, although the manner in which Book II of the *Novum Organum* breaks off makes one assume that he had not been careful enough. Bacon was an encyclopedist; he was convinced from his readings that to rule was to transform given nature into a reasonably comfortable home for rational man. This would be for Bacon the finest tribute possible to the human race. Nation for Bacon was the middle axiom between the universal *humanitas* and the lonely singular human specimen. It was through human life on earth that the universal humanitas, or universal nation, could be induced. He maintained that one need only compare the state of man in India during his times and the state of man in England to see that "Man can be as god to man."

In the spirit of the philosophers of nature in his time, Bacon used the old Greek distinction between the visible and the invisible in nature. He wrote that the visible raw nature was paralleled by a latent physical law that man must discover in order to be able to bend the phenomena to his human bidding. *The social scene was simply some more of the visible nature,* and Bacon wrote that one must analyze the social and political scene around oneself in exactly the same manner one would analyze any other natural phenomena. Behind any political or social state of affairs there lurked invisible but inevitable laws of nature; these laws must be understood if one would grasp the significance of these social or political events and be able to manipulate them to his own ends.

People were the raw material from which the political state would be constructed. This raw material must be understood in terms of its natural latent laws if it would be controlled. As the raw material of the culture, the people were the most precious resource that the culture possessed. Marx calls to our attention how Bacon warned that healthy bodies and spirits of men must serve in the infantry to save the nation. It was the task of the culture to care well for these resources or else lose the advantage of their power.

Bruno had continually written of the double nature of all facts. No fact could be looked at as flat and absolute in itself; for from the one nature must emerge two aspects of that thing. The other aspect of it is the latent chain of hidden causes in the physical world. Materialized, this interplay presented facts within the context of the society. Each fact was named and it was valued, and thereby it was defined for use. Bacon saw well, as did the other philosophers of nature of his time, that one web after another was woven by the human intelligence and was then superimposed upon concrete physical process. Bacon writes that on the subject of the political web he would use his own advice and remain silent. Yet in Book II of the *Novum Organum* he states that the politics of his time were unforgivably corrupt.

As far as the natural sciences are concerned, Bacon held that man must sweep aside all the webs and look behind them. There is an important difference here between Bacon and Bruno. Bruno wrote that the simple observation of the facts was only one way of analyzing the facts. Bruno taught that reflection upon the facts would yield valid insights about facts if and only if the mind had been cleared of all previous cultural conditioning and put in the scientific posture. Bacon, on the other hand, thought that re-formed simple observation must be followed by recording and classifying and that the climb to conjecture must be monitored each step of the way by external steps. Each conjecture thus obtained must be tested with factual experiment before one could proceed to any further reflection upon the problem.

For Bacon, then, the webs would have to be removed very carefully and a chart made of just how this had been done. Only small portions of the web were to be taken down at any one time, and only under the strict supervision of a prescribed method. As one continued to study the construction of the web, one would gain insight into the organ of intelligence that had constructed the web. This was human intelligence for Bacon, and when this was generalized it became the unity of nature. This axiom of axioms was called God, because in Bacon's time and place there was nothing else he could call it.

The axiom of axioms, when tested pragmatically in the social and the political arena, seemed to Bacon to meet the common man's need to give his meagre life a meaning. Bacon would only object to this sort of image of the divine insofar as it crippled men for serving their state and their leaders or insofar as it blocked the investment by the common people in the political community, which *they* must build and sustain.

As previously noted, Bacon saw three kingdoms: the kingdom of nature, the kingdom of God, and the kingdom of man. The doctrine of the coincidence of contraries would hold that the contraries can be integrated through the middle term, either nature and God through man, or God and man through nature, or nature and man through God. Here we have the logic of Plato, the theory of the included middle that leads to generalization; a man, as created by God, and again as animal nature, would yield the generalizations *heaven* and *earth*. Heaven and earth can be integrated through the middle term *existence*. This leads to the generalizations, *civil* and *ecclesiastical*. These can be integrated by the middle term *politics,* and the contraries of this are "the church" and "the state." These can be joined by the term *empire*.

The eye and the ear of man are insatiable. What these senses experience determines the actions of the hand and the mouth. Bacon states repeatedly that *the state need not fear the quantity of knowledge; it is the quality of knowledge which should be the concern of the state.* Contented men are men who are given materials for these insatiable senses. Knowledgeable human beings would be content rather than frustrated. The workings of nature can be observed by curious men, and the ears can be made content with the parallel roar of the factories that glorify God. Evil does not generate in a culture where the *first causes* are understood as beyond the grasp of common men. The waxen wings of the senses will not soar men to heresy if they are sobered by the proper moral text of a good religion and the proper work assignment in an industrialized state.

Wonder is more akin to contemplation than to mere sense. It

need not be feared. Every sun carries with itself its own shadow. Wonder brings with it broken or imperfect knowledge. Science is of fragmentary knowledge. Monarchs, however, are inspired and have a more perfect knowledge. Charity on their part can support science of the natural world in the service of their flock and the strength of their existential nation. *The monarch, in Bacon's view, is to be transmuted into the learned governor; a new nature is to be grafted onto the old.*

The learned governor will be the finest ruler. He will have judgment as to when and what to resolve, given a set of circumstances. Immersion in the problems of government of all the natural resources of the state is the forte of the learned governor. The people of a state are great natural resources to the state. The learned governor knows this and, with charity and good will, he sets the example for them. As scientists imitate particular natures, the man who governs will imitate the unity of nature. "The facts surrounding the choices Fate makes in kings (as one observes their manners) is not discussed by me here in this work." By contrast, the learned governor is a universal man and teaches his people to serve the world. The man who labors only with books and ideas has a defect and weakness in his character. One must not only be literate and studious enough to be able to understand, but must also be able to *act out his duty to the state and to mankind.* It would seem that he who serves only his own state and not the state of man does not do enough. *Man can be as a god to man.* When Bacon notes the way of life that prevails in some countries, he concludes that literate and informed men have a duty there.

Analysis of the latent political process caused Bacon to teach the following: The king and the priest and the philosopher all come together in the learned governor. The "mere politiques" refer all matters to their own fortunes and do not understand their duty to the general welfare. "Philosophers know enough to follow rich men because they know what they need but the rich men do not know enough to follow philosophers," writes Bacon. "It is always meet to submit to the occasion although not to the person." To this he adds, "It is reason to yield to him with thirty legions, according to Caesar."

Using a lawyer's logic Bacon deduces the Christian industrial state as follows: One understands God best from two aspects, power and wisdom, which are manifested by love. This love of God is manifested by his creation of man and of the world of nature for man. The power and wisdom of God filter slowly down into the spirits and internal laws of human structures. Through prudence, man demonstrates the mortal version of godly love, which co-ordinates the power and wisdom which God has provided unto him. The being of God is to men the same as the knowing of God's works. It is through sensible and material laws. These laws from the view of the creature are hidden. Humans name that which they cannot see. There is great confusion in names and words. Men have lost sight of the search for laws, for which the names were given in first place.

We must go back to the search for the laws. If we lose sight of universality or the philosophia prima, then all progress will stop. The challenge is to find what God has hidden and not to babble in many names about what is mere appearances. The laws behind the appearance will free man to become a co-creator with the Divine. God gave man the reasonable faculty in order that man might style himself in the image of God.

As the man who marries empiricism to rationalism with Charity for human life as his witness, Bacon cautions: We must go beyond a science in order to analyze it, but this does not mean that we become insulated in our own little intellectual worlds and ignore the true world which is great and common. We should begin with doubt and end in certainty, when we reason from sensations of the external objects that God gave us. We should not begin in certainty and end up with impossibilities. "Knowledge as a good spouse affords us generations of fruit and comfort as a result of our applying ourselves to the phenomena of rest and motion."

Wisdom is distinguishable from learning. Learning is acquired, but wisdom is original in God. To glorify God men must take it as duty to seek out His law. Therefore, *it is the duty of men to explore nature*. However, the inquisition of truth is necessary in order that nature be explored. "The Savior demonstrated his power to subdue ignorance before he showed his power to subdue nature." First He planted faith in the simple people and later he sent the inspired men.

Learning and philosophy serve religion in two ways. They demonstrate the will of God by analyzing words for reasons and rules. They also demonstrate the power of God, by building a second nature upon his works. "You err, not knowing the will of the Scriptures nor the power of God," quotes Bacon.

Bacon tempers his science of nature with prudence toward social change: Men should not try to *be* God, although they should *imitate* God. We can but approximate the Law of God. Our honors and achievements are human honors and achievements. Men must give ears to the laws and to religions as best as they are discerned. Otherwise there will be anarchy and confusion. If men proceed in the understanding of the notions of religion, policy, and morality, then they have the material with which to be learned governors. Although one can easily see that "to receive a prophet in the name of a prophet is to receive a prophet's reward," those who govern should teach civil merit and moral virtue. The temperate use of prerogative is very important. The informed sovereign promotes a learned sovereignty. The powerful sovereign's needs are few and simple. Bacon reminds us that Alexander kept Hope for himself and gave away Wealth.

In order to set up the desired throne in the soul of a man, one must make sure that that man has some knowledge and learning. The highest part of the mind is the commandment of reason and belief and understanding, and this comes from knowing and learning. The faith and conscience of man should not be commanded over by those who are detestably tied to pleasurable bloating of themselves. The just and lawful sovereignty over men's understanding is through the force of truth which is rightly interpreted. One understands rightly interpreted truth through the *argument from contraries*. This is divine sovereignty. "The priesthood has been in competition with empire because they have been carried by learning while some kings have been carried only by armies."

Bacon reassures his monarch that non-noble men are totally mortal: knowledge and learning can be seen to be good in themselves; they surpass all the other pleasures in nature. In knowledge, satisfaction is never enough. Appetite and satisfaction are constantly interchanging. Men can soar to the heavens through learning but they cannot soar in body. Monuments of wit and learning are more durable than monuments of power and lands. Immortality is gained through memory, fame and celebration, by inseminating the coming ages of men.

As to moral and private virtue, the man who meditates upon the universal laws of nature will see the earth with its inhabitants as an ant hill. Note Bruno's words in *De Immenso* about logically observing the earth from the moon: "Notice how Britain is condensed to a small point and the very narrow Italy is condensed into a thin and short hair" (IV, 3). Man will have no fear of death as he understands the corruptible nature of all things. If a man understands goodness, then he can acquire the *way* of goodness. This only holds in moral affairs, for Bacon. For Bruno, it holds both in moral affairs and in natural affairs. For Bacon, most men tend to hide their weakest aspects. They attempt to operate only in the one-sided way of their spontaneous successes. The learned man is the man who will not settle for this way of life. The learned man re-arranges his own powers, using the spontaneous powers which he has to acquire strengths in the aspects where he needs to acquire strength.

Bacon describes the monarch so as to "praise" the office. One has dignity in his command of others only insofar as those others have dignity. A man who rules brutes is not a ruler at all. Commonwealths have a sweet dignity when they command over the wills of men, and not merely over the services of men. But to command over the reasonable and those of understanding is the greatest dignity of all.

The dispensations of times will determine the gradations of light or reason which will be material to the suppositions of belief. In one light the measure, "He who is not with us, is against us," is held to be the most prudent. In another light, "He is not against us; therefore he is with us," might be taken as the correct measure. It was said that "the robe of the Savior was without seam," and therefore we would understand that differences in religious rites do not have to entail essential differences in private morality. A common morality can be generated from a common belief which is made manifest in a myriad of diverse habits. The more one recedes from the simple religious insights, the more confused his conclusions become. Similarly, in Bacon's theory of knowledge, the further one recedes from the common sense object, the more confused one becomes, unless one is "guided and guarded" in the faculties of thought. The state should keep the faith simple, and not far-removed from human experience. In this way the state religion will need few symbolic aids.

Bacon wrote that a scientific project must be undertaken to document the *total* history of the life of man. This history shall be written in a language fitted to the "light" of the times. The Scriptures are methodical and again they are in-solution. Custom and habit materialize in times, and times are dependent on the gradation of light dispensed to man. Therefore, customs must continue in deference to excellence. "But, that upon which knowledge has depended, will continue also as it does not fail." Each nation and each time has a duty to do its share, according to its power and understanding. The record of human achievement should be carefully maintained. There should be an actual gathering and study of human work in all the fields of past and present human achievement. There should also be a record of human reflections and musing upon the human conditions and the human achievements in the past, and of the present, and in imagining the future. There should be careful and exact inquiry of nature by man. This latter activity includes the divine in nature, the faith in the law of natural law, or theology. It will also include the inquiry into the causes in nature, physics, and metaphysics. It will include the production of natural effects through experiments, theories of physics, and theories of metaphysics. This activity of inquiry by man into nature will include also the study of man.

Bacon points out that the study of man involves the study both of individual men and of the civil condition. Man, as individual, has a general nature that can be investigated through two aspects, the mind and the body. Mind has two aspects, the soul and the faculties. Human faculties of mind have two aspects, the moral and the rational. As a result of these faculties of human nature, we have natural philosophy and philosophy of morality. In respect to the generalizing nature of individual man, moral philosophy has to do with eliciting the nature of the good. As the nature of the good relates to the individual man (thinking as an individual), it has to do with the cultivation of his own mind. Apart from the individual human and his search for the cultivation of his own mind, there is the aspect of his duty which grows out of the individual's generalizing, from the nature of the good to the nature of duty in general. Here Bacon retains Bruno's materialized logic of contraries.

Study of the civil condition is the study of man as congregate. The civil condition has three aspects from which inquiry can approach it. These aspects are the activities of civil men, the organization of the congregation, and the nature of the congregation. The nature of the congregation or government is immersed in material considerations. The governed and the governor are contraries. The government which is the coincidence of these two is obscure and invisible. Human government, a social nature, is an effect produced by humanity from natural philosophy. It is the contrary to divine philosophy. These two natural congregations coincide in *philosophia prima*, which is the result of human knowledge based upon science. Here, too, the coincidence of contraries is used.

Bacon clearly calls for a science of polity for the maintenance of republics: "As for the social congregation or human government, the laws are the most public aspect of it. My complaint is though that these laws are either written by philosophers or by lawyers. They should be written by statesmen. The lawyer is not a lawmaker." The law has two aspects: there is the platform of justice, and then there is the implementation of justice. The implementation of justice must deal with the study of means of and impediments to execution of the laws. The laws are to be devised, delivered, and written down. They should communicate for the "meum and teum" nature of the state. "Therefore the state must supervise the implementation of justice through administration procedures. *I have begun a work describing the proper manner of this.*" He goes on: "The civil law is not very often designed for the government where it governs. Enough said about this here. I do not intend to mix matters of action with matters of learning in this work." The mixing of matters of action and matters of learning is advocated by Bacon in many places. He often calls for the "whole man" in natural sciences, a man not too rash and not too contemplative. Yet, for fear of sounding "dangerous", Bacon here cloaks the whole man.

"Time has a propriety, as its nature, and so time works to the disclosure of the truth. We are moving closer and closer to the truth. The first two periods, the Greek and the Roman, will be surpassed by this *third period of ours*." Reason and will are the two contraries of the civil knowledge. The light of nature gives sense induction, reason, and argument, through which the laws of nature are known to men. "This first state of mankind is sufficient to check vice but is not sufficient to inform men of their duty." There is the control of man as instinctual creature, through the powers he has by natural light. This can only yield posit, though. *Posita juris* is reasonable, but reason is not enough. For administration one needs the authority of *placita juris*.

The *placita juris* is that authority based upon acceptance by re-formed understanding. No science can grow unless the implications of its fruits are discovered and gathered and subjected to the inductive procedures and the inductive tests for usefulness to the civil state. In this way the human mind may exercise the proper authority over the kingdom of natural things.

The "learned governor" is the coincident of human curiosity and national habit. He is the reflection of the flow of time and does not attempt to live the future in the present, or the past in the present. The learned governor *lives* the present in the present, with an astute eye open to both the past and the future. In this way the learned governor *illuminates the appropriate occasion* from alternative possibilities. He operates with a firm benevolence, between piety and wisdom. His finest judgments are made with his eye upon prudence. These ideas and their mode of expression were all discussed in Bacon's day. They are the ancient teachings in the form of the new materialism that was spoken loudly in Bruno. In Bacon and more cautious writers, the materialism was cloaked by a license for theological Revelation.

(The material quoted from Bacon in this chapter is from the *Advancement of Learning,* reading for the most part with the Oxford edition of 1960. The same points are often repeated in the *Novum Organum.*)

CHAPTER THREE

LEARNED GOVERNOR

1. Regulated Observation
2. Corrected Anticipation
3. Legitimate Interpretation

1.

REGULATED OBSERVATION

THE WHOLE TOPIC of "learning" is analyzed by Bacon through a study and critique of the ways and means used in his own times for making knowledge-claims. Bacon says that he is going to give refutations of these ways and means, and show that they must be re-formed in order to yield a new way and a new means that will be a system founded on the lawful and orderly balancing of the common senses with the intellect. This new way will be an intellectual operation that will find the "middle axiom" as the first goal. The middle axiom that lies between the common sense and the highest intellectual axiom is the link that has been missing. Rationalists have flown, straightway, to the highest axioms, but without demonstrating method through which those highest axioms can be seen to be arrived at legitimately. Other men have been rashly empirical, and have tied their hours and their experiments to one accidentally-noted phenomenon without any effort to integrate this phenomenon into a just and orderly investigation of its latent law.

Bacon felt that *utility for the culture* might be the badly needed guideline that would trim the flight of the rationalist and correct the myopia of the rash empiric. Bacon makes the analogy of the rash empiric with the ant; the rationalist he compares to the spider. He suggests that what we need to do is to imitate the bee. The bee avails itself of its own power to transform what it takes in and thus produces *useful* honey. He compares the good university to a bee hive, which should be prepared to shelter and provide for bees so that they might work in peace. This would be a far cry from the academy of webs, or the ant hill of alchemy. It was the stable balance of the two methods which was called for. Bacon says, "I have wedded the empirics to the rationalists in proper proportion."

83

This new system that Bacon wanted for the scientific harnessing of nature, was to be used also for the governing of the state. He had seen the ultimate in tyranny by absolute rulers as against the slow struggle for the amelioration of this tyranny through the middle position between the ruler and the people. This middle position between the ruler and the ruled was a representative body called the Parliament. Bacon served in this body for years. As an encyclopedist he had wanted to serve in that parliament which represented the possibility of support for the building of re-formed schools. In this way Bacon saw himself as a whole man, a learned governor for the scientific method in both the natural and social fields.

The ruler of the *nation* should be a parallel to the ruler of *nature*. The ruler of nation was empowered by God to lead the human, earthly flock. But the ruler of nation was also limited by the teachings of that God. The Scriptures gave the mandates for the ruler of the kingdom to follow. Where these mandates were in-solute, the re-formed philosopher and the re-formed theologian would offer their best to the ruler, who would then reflect and meditate upon it, and finally emerge (as God would inspire him as Vicar) with the proper exegesis of the in-solute Biblical mandate.

For Bacon the learned governor moved between the *births of wit* and the *births of occasion*. This middle position was *the birth for the times*. For in government as well as in science, untimely practice had brought only bloodshed and human torches, tied to the stake of authority. In civil matters, the new scientific observation of the natural sciences would have to be employed. After we place Bacon in the political context of his times, let us look, with regulated observation, at those times as Bacon lived them.

During Bacon's flourish in Tudor England under Elizabeth, there emerges a rather mature and urbane attitude on the part of the monarch toward members of the populace and their personal lives. It is an earmark of the Elizabethan period that each man's soul is actually his own to save, so long as he *does not threaten* the person of the monarch or swear political allegiance to a foreign power. Some of this is lost in the reign of James. Bacon accommodates the use of the royal prerogative to the needs of James. James also had children, and the marriages and possible marriages of these children complicated the political picture, as the unions, through the marriages of royal children, with royalty that was Roman in faith, again became a problem. This had not been a problem for the court in the time of Elizabeth.

After the reign of Elizabeth there was no longer the steady hand of Burleigh. Robert Cecil was not of the same temperament as his father, and entered into political intrigues that the older Burleigh would have avoided. There was not the rapport between Robert Cecil and the monarch James that there had been between Elizabeth and Burleigh.

Bacon knew the political terrain as well as the palm of his hand during the reign of Elizabeth. The Essex-Anthony Bacon security office often had more information than did Walsingham. Such was not the case after James took power. For Bacon, it was only by way of extending his skills in adjustment and James' need to have him use his political influence with the men who sat in the Commons, that power could be sought. This Bacon did, along with performing acts of camouflage and expediency for the favorites of James to gain recognition. However, he was never really on the inside. The court of James was not at all of the same fabric as that of Elizabeth I. The insiders were not men of politics, but men of vanity and personal charm who could provide for James the emotional and psychological support he needed. The visions for empire were not there. Rather, it was the vision for integration that was there: James was concerned mostly with fitting into the world of monarchies as a full-fledged member. It had been quite a step from the throne of Scotland to the throne of "Great Brittany". It was quite a step from the role of a monarch of Scotland to the role of the monarch of England as seen by Henry VII, Henry VIII, and Elizabeth I.

Bacon, as was his habit and as was required by his logic, adapted to the needs of the new monarch. From this vantage point, Bacon pushed the definition of the royal prerogative to its fullest possible limit, for practical political obedience. The survival of *nation* depended on sustaining the King. In his theory of knowledge, Bacon would not have allowed for this straining of the royal prerogative in nature; nature is not unruly.

In order to be understood as a serious thinker, Bacon must be seen in the terms of the two reigns, with their distinctive features. In turn, the two reigns must be seen within the wider context of the international conditions of their times. The highest value for Bacon was *the adjustment of the simple observation* to a carefully worked out logical plan for snaring an interpretation of the process under study. Used in a regulated way, the simple observation could play a predictive role. Therefore, this simple observation must be adjusted very carefully, so that the information that it carried could reveal a latent configuration. This was the way in which Bacon thought nature and nation could undergo scientific analysis. Man should live in a *planned* nation, hewn out of planned natures—animate and inanimate and human.

It is a mistake to call Bacon an empiricist. For him, the actual significance of the particular case was in its dormant configuration and the way in which this latent configuration was lawfully locked into the rest of the latent configurations. The pattern of these latent configurations was the law of nature. These latent configurations were the subsidiary laws of nature and the middle latent ground between the manifest particular case and the ultimate unchanging law of nature. In his statecraft, Bacon used this same model. Actual events and particular actions were the most valuable when understood *as mere clues* to an underlying process and configuration of motives and aims and latent power plays.

When Bacon sorely needed funds, and entreaties to his uncle, Lord Burleigh, were not yielding results, Bacon would write his uncle letters assuring Burleigh that he, Bacon, had only the aim of intellectual power. He assured Burleigh that the empire which he coveted was the empire of all knowledge and not the political empire of the English throne. Bacon repeats this statement in his *Essays*. He states that he has only "moderate civil ends" and "vast contemplative ends." He states that "philanthropia" is his goal.

This was in keeping with the aversion that Tudor England felt for the French word "politique", which stood for mere craft and cunning in the royal circles, and was not popular in England. Therefore, in attempting to fashion a concept which reflected the birth of the new utilitarian English, Bacon adapted that concept, *philanthropia,* which seemed the most progressive for existential government. As time goes on, Bacon seems to settle for the word "knowledge", which is one aspect of *philosophia prima*. The other aspect of *philosophia prima* is "faith." Together, these two human efforts constitute "natural philosophy". Natural philosophy has two aspects, causal and effective. In Bacon, from the "causal" frame of reference, knowledge matures in the systematic inquiries of physics (material and efficient) and metaphysics (formal and final). Note that, for Bacon, final causes were considered as part of the dignity of human knowledge *not* in physics, but in matters *beyond* physics. Note that where we above have specified "systematic inquiries", Bacon took the time to explain that by this idea, he meant merely "speculations". The religious tone of the day demanded this distinction. Systematic bodies of statements, dealing with Truth, were seen as reserved for the catechisms of faith. Bacon wanted catechisms for utilitarian pursuit of physical nature. These were not acceptable in his times. Libraries were acceptable, but no hint of books containing recorded truths about nature went without an inquisition. The encyclopedic tradition was implemented only later, with the political sanction.

From the "effective" frame of reference, knowledge matures in the systematic *production* of effects. Manipulation of *natural effects* yielded *scientific effects,* such as experimental physics and its written history, or experimental social science and its written history. The physics had a dual aspect, technological and mechanical. (Bacon did not promote the method of theoretical physics. As a correction to the fruitless metaphysics of his times, Bacon played down the "jump to remote axioms".) The social sciences had a dual aspect also. The society was to be studied once from the aspect of a man as an aggregate (a particular nature), and again from the aspect of men as a congregation. For Bacon, this congregation or society represented a new nature, grafted onto the natural world and designed out of the raw materials of particular human natures. The systematic study of this new nature, the human congregation, was civil knowledge. The aim here was a rational analysis and re-arrangement of the congregation in terms of the most useful modes of human life. Here Bacon could be understood as a precursor of Marx. Bacon's rationale for the infant English nation (as she had fought for survival ever since the reign of Henry VII) seemed to work, through the nineteenth century. This totally materialistic and utilitarian view of human congregation in English society was recognized by Engels.

Bacon's report of the human scene as being primarily materialistic and technological holds that human nature, when scientifically progressed to its rightful place, will rule over inanimate, natural process. It seems that man is again "king of the Cosmos", and the universe again becomes anthropomorphic. The medieval image is intact, but this time the anthropomorphic universe is the one actually created by the genius of men. It is the human world that has completely subdued the rational cosmos by virtue of wresting from this silent cosmos her secret laws of operation. Anthropomorphic man only posited unruly nature in his infancy.

Giordano Bruno, in the *Spaccio,* had analyzed social concepts to ascertain whether or not they belonged in Heaven as patterns for earth. They were found to be relatively qualified, depending upon what concepts came before Jove to plead for a chair in Heaven. One by one Bruno demonstrates that their relationship to other social concepts must be explicated before one could decide whether or not they were vices or virtues. Each social concept was seen to be capable of functioning unwisely, and, in this way, these concepts were vices. Each concept was seen as capable of linking up with other concepts in an unfortunate way for human welfare, thus becoming ineligible to be called a virtue. Bruno wrote this dialogue in England in 1584, and Bacon draws heavily from it.

Bacon uses his *Essays* to place these social concepts in an existential milieu, in which they are demonstrated as being useful or harmful to men in society. As in Bruno, the social concepts emerge as relatively valuable, depending on the *way* in which they are *used* in situational contexts.

Bacon, in the *Essays,* states that actually his writings deal with matters already known. He writes, "the word is late, but the thing is ancient." Yet he feels that each age can add evidence to previous assertions, and he proceeds to document some of his insights which corroborate well-taken assertions. Mostly, he uses the Old Testament speakers, and the Romans, as examples of some well-placed observations which seem to hold up in the experience of his own time.

In the essay *Of Truth,* Bacon says that truth is pursued, known,

and enjoyed when mankind is in a state of goodness. Faith has to
do with the enjoyment of truth, and "it is heaven upon earth, to
have a man's mind move in charity, rest in providence, and turn
upon the poles of truth." Bacon says that "clear and round dealing"
in service to the *honorable* aspect of human nature enables truth
to be approached in the three modes, through practical accom-
modation of a pluralistic ethical manifestation of truth: the theological truth, scientific truth, and the truth of civil business. He
states that "a mixture of a lie always brings pleasure." Then, he
says that "the mixture of a lie as an alloy has its uses but does em-
base." We see this in Bruno:

> . . . Majesty, Glory, Decorum, Dignity, Honor, and other com-
> panions, with their courts are here in Heaven. These *by first choice*
> ordinarily move about the areas of Simplicity, Truth, and similar
> others, and sometimes, *by force of necessity,* move in the area of
> Dissimulation and similar others, *which, by accident, can be the
> refuge* of virtues. (*Spaccio,* Imerti, p. 82, my italics)

And Bacon writes (in his essay, "Of Simulation and Dissimulation"):

> The best composition and temperature is to have openness in fame
> and opinion; secrecy in habit; dissimulation in seasonable use; and
> a power to feign, if there be no remedy.

It would weight this work down too heavily to show all the ideas
from Bruno's writings that reappear in Bacon. One needs only to
read Bruno in order to see that they are heavy throughout. Bacon's
own words are as follows:

> Wherefore I do conclude this part of moral knowledge, concerning
> the culture and regiment of the mind; wherein if any man, con-
> sidering the parts thereof which I have enumerated, do judge that my
> labour is but to collect into an art or science that which hath been
> previously determined by others, as matter of common sense and
> experience, he judgeth well. (*A.L.,* II, xxii, 16)

But then Bacon adds that although he uses the work of others, he
is different from them, as Philocrates had said he differed from
Demosthenes. Philocrates had said that he drank wine while Demosthenes drank water (*ibid.*). Here, Bacon appears to be admitting that he depressed his logical aim enough to be good-natured
about the necessary providential tempering of inquiry (see *A.L.,*
II, xxv, 8).

The quest for and the enjoyment of Truth might well entail ethically limber and ambidextrous models which demonstrated truth as shadow demonstrates light. This was a prevalent view during Bacon's time. Bruno had written that knowledge was essentially recognizable from falsehood, because true knowledge yielded useful works that canceled out shadowy knowledge. Bacon (after living through the burning of Bruno) decided that "the customary must come first, although that which knowledge brings, will never fail." In his essay on death, Bacon agrees with the philosophers of nature of his times in the mood of Epicurus. He states that "It is as natural to die as to be born." He adds that a man whose mind is in proper order, does not see sadness in death.

In regard to unity in religion, Bacon wrote that quarrels and divisions in religion were unknown to heathens. Constancy of belief, rather than preoccupation with rites, would sustain unity. Unity and uniformity are needed so that an outward peace provided by the church could give a peace in the conscience. Contradictions are in words only, for terms govern the meaning. Unity should not cost us the laws needed in existential society nor proper laws of charity. "There be two swords amongst Christians, the spiritual and the temporal; and both have their due office and place in the maintenance of religion. But we may not take up the third sword, which is Mahomet's sword, or like unto it; that is, to propagate religion by wars or by sanguinary persecutions to force consciences; except it be in cases of overt scandal, blasphemy, or intermixture of practice against the state . . .," such as putting the sword in the hands of the people. For "government . . . is the ordinance of God." It is monstrous to put the temporal sword of religion in the hands of the people. Here, Bacon sees the practice of religion as an instrument of state. It is a societal glue which binds human beings to their governor through obedience and through common understandings of human destiny.

Bacon wrote of Fortune: "though she be blind, yet she is not invisible." Each man can see where he is going if he is prudent enough to look ahead. A man builds his own fortune by learning that virtue is dual. Fortune is gained through learning how to appreciate the secret and hidden virtues, "the wheels of his mind keep way with the wheels of his fortune." Open virtue brings reputation as a man places his thought outside himself, but this man does not go his own way. Bacon points out that "extreme lovers of country are not so fortunate." It is implied here that if they do not bend, they may be sacrificed.

Bacon demonstrates again his eclectic attitude toward life and society. There seems to be no excuse for a man not to learn how to balance both private dealings and his reputation to his own advantage. Again, being very practical, Bacon writes that usury will always be part of society because "men are so hard of heart," although Bacon admits that "it is against nature for money to beget money." He quotes the Scriptures: "In the sweat of thy face shalt thou eat bread—not in the sweat of another's face." Those who lend money should be licensed and carefully watched to make sure they enable the economy rather than disable it, Bacon suggests. Usury can help an economy if properly handled. On the other hand, there are marked disadvantages possible.

Bacon learned that negotiations could be more effective by letter than by speech. Also, a third party should be used. In this way one has witnesses to his position and possibly actual aid. In tender, delicate matters, an eye-to-eye contact works very well, if one is able to work this power. Bacon wrote that dealing with men who want something is more profitable than dealing with men who have all the power they need. In order to "work" a man, one must know that man very well. One must study him and understand intimately his weaknesses and his strengths. Here, Bacon is quite frank about the fact that he believes that man, like any other natural object, can only be commanded if one approaches him by finding his Achilles' heel and his style of power.

Men who are followed by costly entourages have "long trains and short wings." All of his life, this was Bacon's condition. However, he learned that there was little real friendship between equals but that friendship flowered between superiors and inferiors. One should never depend entirely on one friend, but, rather, place himself in choice of friends where he can help himself best. Telling tales to men of equal rank is a good way of finding out much, and then one is able to have a tidbit of value for his friend of superior power. "The valley best locates the hill." One standing in the wings is in a position to assess the action on the stage better than those on the stage.

Bacon wrote in regard to suits that expertise is second to learn-edness. Study must be "bounded by experience." One who well deliberates these matters understands the essential, hidden me-chanics of the problem, and also understands the societal ability to deal with those hidden mechanics. Studies "perfect nature, and are perfected by experience." You should always "ask more than is reasonable, that you may get no less," was Bacon's recommenda-tion from experience. Suspicions are a problem of one's logic, says Bacon. These suspicions, he has found, arise out of "missing" facts. Never smother these suspicions, he teaches. Rather, con-front those concerned. In this way, some facts are always picked up, and facts are what is missing.

In all discourse one should try to attain the middle road be-tween being wearisome and being blunt. Discretion is the acme of discourse. Bacon goes on, "As we see in beasts, that those that are weakest in the course, are yet nimblest in the turn; as it is betwixt the greyhound and the hare." To penetrate and feign at being pene-trated is the conversant posture Bacon thinks is best.

Bacon wrote that he found riches to be the "baggage of virtue." He uses a Roman reference and agrees that "impedimenta" would be a better word. An army is deterred by its baggage, and the vir-tuous are deterred by their riches. The only possible value of riches, for Bacon, is to use them as tools to enable one to do some good, as says Cicero. Bacon also quotes Solomon that to choose riches is to give up innocence. Inheritance and foundations are regenerative insofar as one is very liberal with another man's wealth. Bacon practiced this. He spent freely to garner all knowl-edge. As for ambition, it should be tempered by the understand-ing of one's duty. A "willing" mind is preferable to an ambitious one. Ambition, if balanced by a good will, is an asset. Bacon sounds like Kant here.

Nature is never extinguished, Bacon taught. It can be hidden and overcome, but in these cases the price is always violence from nature. Hardened custom which causes the least conflict with na-ture will endure best. This means that training is of the essence, and that practice (hard and tough) is in order. There are cases of fortitude when man, with one powerful thrust, is capable of throwing off his chains. If one doesn't have this power, he bends.

Bacon teaches that one "should imitate Aesop's damsel and avoid the occasion or frequent it," in order to become desensitized to it. Books are to be "swallowed, tasted or chewed." Study that which balances one's behavior best, he decided.

Bacon noticed that great men have personal power and usually stand alone. In factions, when the leader is gone, division sets in, and the next in line becomes the leader. Factions within a state can be pernicious if they do not keep rhythm with "the prime mover" of the government.

In acting on ceremony, one should balance the formal and the familiar. "A wise man will take more opportunity than he finds." "He that considers the wind, will not sow, and he that considers the clouds will not reap." A man's behavior should be definitive but a bit obscure, "like clothes, not too binding but admitting exercise and motion." "The common people admire the lowest virtues and some admire the middle virtues. The highest virtues are just not known by them at all. It is the *appearance* of virtue which goes best with them." "Fame is like a river that carries the light weight and buries the heavy." So the common people praise that which is inferior. One should use praise toward one's superiors also as a teaching device. One should praise the throne (not the man) in order to demonstrate to those who hold it the duty that goes with it.

Properly ranked seats of honor are: First, among rulers, are the founders of states or commonwealths; then, lawgivers. Next, liberators against invaders, and then defenders of empires. Last place goes to "patres" who reign justly. In subjects, honor rank runs like this: First, the "sharers of cares"; next, the "duces belli"; third, the "gratiosi" (favorites who help the ruler and do not harm the people); and the fourth, "negotiis pares" or those equal to the business of great place and recognized and used by the monarch. There is another honor, which is rare and placed among the greatest of honors: it is the sacrifice of oneself to death or danger for the good of one's country.

I believe that Bacon felt that he belonged to this last and highest type of honorable men. After serious study of his life and work, one would tend to agree with him. Although he did avoid direct confrontation almost always, he flirted with disaster time after time. Bacon was probably one of the most successfully "discrete" men in history, when one takes into consideration the game of politics he played and the tenor of the times in which he played the political game.

All of these suggestions by Bacon reflect the attitudes of other writers on the subject. But *Bacon is speaking from experience and verifying them.*

Vainglory Bacon described through the device of Aesop: "The fly sat upon the axletree of the chariot wheel, and said, What a dust do I raise!" There were men like this in the states; Bacon described them as men of faction, violence, and noisy reputation. They used the media of war, books, negotiations between two princes, naval enterprises, and business enterprises. This does not mean that these pursuits in themselves are only instruments of vainglory. They are not. Men of discretion use these same media with good taste and in service to the state.

There is another side to this for Bacon. Many men do very little very solemnly and seem to be wise. They secret much and are actually hiding very little. As to friendship, Bacon wrote that "whoever is delighted with solitude is either a wild beast or a god." Solitude, though, need not be the mere rejection of men; it can be the change from men to the muses. For talk can be merely a "tinkling cymbal." Even a king needs a friend, someone who can share his cares. The Roman example of love of one man for another, especially among the Roman princes, is offered here by Bacon. One needs more than wife and children; one needs the love of a friend. Joys are re-doubled, and sorrows are cut in half, through friends of good will. As in nature, and known by the alchemists, natural bodies are *strengthened* by union and weakened by being torn apart from each other, when there is a natural sympathy between them.

Affections of men need the balance of exchange through another, in order that excess be lost and deprivation be supplied. Minds of men need their match in order to remain balanced. Counsel from a friend, whether agreeable at first or not, helps to keep a man's understanding in critical balance. "Friendship affords harmony in the affections and good judgment in the understanding." He quotes the ancients who hold that "a friend is another self," and adds that actually a friend is much more than that. A friend will finish what a man leaves undone, says Bacon. A man can only speak as a husband to a wife or as a father to a son. A friend can do better than that for a man. A man can hardly sing his own praises. But a friend can say what should be said about a man's accomplishments. Bacon lays down the role for friendship: "Where a man cannot fitly play his own part, if he have not a friend, he may quit the stage." Here again, we see Bacon as nakedly eclectic, and perhaps franker than any of us like to admit.

The kingdom of heaven is always compared to a mustard seed rather than to a large gem. The greatest kingdom, then, would be that one which was the most fertile of the most useful and sorely needed materials for raising up the human welfare. In this way, the state will grow and grow, not merely in number but in well-cared-for numbers. A state could not be peopled by "the lion's whelp" *and* the "ass between burdens." The common people should be more than merely the gentlemen's laborers. Otherwise, the nation's body is diseased, and therefore the nation is not sound. This seems brutally sombre. One would prefer to think of a nation providing for its people for more altruistic reasons. However, Bacon is simply blunt about the truth.

Bacon reminds us that the trunk of the monarchy bears the branches and the leaves. The nation should be aware of wrongs in its body. The body of the nation should not be feverish and restrained. It should be in good health. A race of men not fit to defend their state make a kingdom anything but great. The macrocosm (the ruler) and the microcosm (the subject) coincide in the organism of nation. Occasion and will coincide in power as wit or knowledge. The state is the occasion, the people its will, and wit or knowledge is its aim.

Power as three-dimensional (act or occasion, will or duty, knowledge or wit) can be discussed from *any one* of these dimensions. In this case *that one* of these dimensions becomes the synthesis of the other two dimensions. Earlier, this was written by Bruno, who materialized the coincidence of contraries of Nicholas of Cusa. This logic is not closed. Each of the three points that represents an aspect of power can be taken as the coincidence of both of the other two points. From Bruno on, the logic is materialized,

and explains the dynamics of human existence in terms of the selection of basic conceptual values. These conceptual values are seen
as being manipulated eclectically to exonerate the state's ideology
in very different situations. *Logic becomes the servant of political
ideology.*

As for adjudication in the state, Bacon says that corruption of
the fountain of justice is worse than corruption of the stream. The
course of the stream is defined by laws. Judges direct the evidence
within these streams, making certain that the material evidence
remains well within the banks of the stream. "One foul sentence is
worse than many foul examples, because foul sentences corrupt
the fountain of justice while foul examples merely corrupt the
stream." The bench is a hallowed place, and a judge should imitate
God.

Bacon uses the Romans and the Old Testament as guides. He
says that "just law and true policy move as one." In other words,
the rule of the nation cannot have integrity on the throne unless
the administration of justice in his state coincides with the policies
from his throne. Bacon reminds us that the lions, which supported
Solomon's throne, were under that throne.

This very point cost Bacon his career, in his conflict with the
lawyer Coke. Bacon thought the royal prerogatives were actually
to be harmonized with the natural prerogatives of men. Royalty
understandably would determine how to arrange the weights. He
taught, in other writings, that the natural prerogatives of men
were those of their natural animality and reason. He also taught
that men should bend, if they were not in a position to assert these
prerogatives at any one time. Men should bend and wait and prepare. It boils down to Bacon's prudence as against Coke's disgusted impatience. For Bacon, timing was of the essence. He
didn't see how it was possible to push for more synchronization of
the wheels of human intelligence with the wheels of natural power
at that time. Bacon himself could have easily switched his whole
attitude and written: The lions under Solomon's throne were the
support of that throne. The man who sits in that throne should
not put undue weight on that throne or the lions will come out and
devour him. Bacon *did not write this* because he was convinced
that the time was not ripe. But it is apparent from his writings on

civil knowledge in the *Advancement of Learning* and in his *Novum Organum* that he understood it well and desired a change to enlightened leadership.

Bacon warns that law can be torturous and that many times emergency laws which are intended to quell treasons are left on the books and become habits. In this way, terror becomes routine. "Times" as well as "matter" must be considered, then, in order to write good law. "Judges", says Bacon, "shall always keep a severe eye upon the matter but show mercy for the man." Bacon means this. He saw men as struggling to express themselves and to fulfill their needs in spite of overwhelming political impediments.

Bacon believed that it was not always an easy matter to find the "prudent path" between piety and intelligence. When a man missed the mark, this was understandable, although the case must be studied carefully to ascertain what this example of trespass might cost the state in stability. Treatment of the man was to be rendered on that basis. So, when Bacon speaks of atheism, he recommends the burning alive of atheists if they are political threats to the stability of the state. Anger in men can only be controlled but not eliminated, Bacon writes. Again he brings in "timing." To wait is the answer, lest one do anything which will be beyond repair. The contraries of "hurt" and "contempt" can be mediated by understanding. One needs a "stout web of honor" and should not be such men "that puts their lives in the sting", as the bee does.

Human experience is all a matter of flux, and yet there is really no novelty being introduced as Bacon saw it. What is discovered is human power to convert nature to utility, because "times" change and inventions are looked for as the human scene is ready for them. He quotes Solomon and uses Plato to make his point. In nature, deluge and earthquake cover up the past. On the human scene, sects and religions cause all the commotion. Speculative heresies really do not hurt the state unless some sect or religion makes an issue of it. "But when the eagle of empire falls, each sparrow takes a feather." Generation gaps bring contrary interests which mechanical arts and merchandising could close. Here Bacon demonstrates again the respect he has for the co-incident of brawn and brain. Together, through training and education, these two human powers can meet as one rational organism and produce a healthy state. Martyrs may be natural signs that the state has abuses to be cleaned up, Bacon offers.

Learned governance entails being able to exquisitely judge the *appropriate* dose of any social concept necessary to a social situation. Learned governance is observation regulated with respect to *external* reference rather than with oneself as reference. Proper diagnostic insight of a social situation will lead to exactly the proper formula or recipe of social concepts needed to treat the situation. Judgment consists in this: recognizing *what* to formulate and finding *the appropriate combination* or ratio of social concepts in order to come up with the needed logical proposition at the right time in the right place. A man who could do this was a learned governor.

Bruno had written about the double nature of the good in each thing. Each thing strived to preserve itself as itself, and again each thing strived to realize its universal role. All bodies had two kinds of motion for Bruno: local motion around its own center and universal motion as it strived to act out its role in the universal scheme of the totality. Bacon repeats this point. "There is formed in everything a double nature of good: the one, as everything is a total in itself; the other, as it is a part or member of a greater body . . ." (*A.L.*, Bk. II, xx, 7) Human duty would have to be understood as having this double nature (*A.L.*, Bk. II, xxi, 1, 2).

2.

CORRECTED ANTICIPATION

L EARNED GOVERNANCE also called for anticipations from the reflective judgment rather than from mere animal anticipation. This is again in complete analogy with the epistemology. As in Bruno, the "regolato sentimento" was the goal for the conduct of human life in both natural and social sciences.

Bacon's own life showed a slow re-formation in his own anticipations from the crown. This led to the self-discipline on Bacon's part which any learned governor (from macrocosm to microcosm, from king to everyman) needed.

Bacon was born in 1560. He was raised as the son of Sir Nicholas Bacon, who was the Lord Keeper to Elizabeth, and Anne Cooke, a lady-in-waiting at the court who was a royal tutor and a daughter of Sir Anthony Cooke, who was also part of the court. Sir Nicholas had four sons, all grown, and was a widower when he was married to Anne Cooke. In the literature there are references to a rumor that Sir Nicholas and Anne Cooke were married to provide a family for Anthony and Francis who were two small sons of Elizabeth by Dudley. These references in the literature are of uneven value.

Elizabeth was very indifferent to his needs for a very long time, and only in the very last days of her reign did she see him personally to a great extent and rely on him. When Elizabeth did use Bacon it was to prosecute traitors, to confiscate papal holdings in England, and to write the crown's rationale for obtaining money from the Parliament. She paid him poorly for his work and ignored most of his lavish gifts to her and his letters begging for recognition as a faithful and willing servant who was entitled to a high post. The literature contains frequently the statement made by Elizabeth to Burleigh after receiving one of Bacon's letters: "I pulled him through Grey's Inn, isn't that enough?"

Most of the works which would be made available to Bacon through his correspondence abroad and at home were of an avant-garde nature for those times, and would not lend themselves to open publication if signatured too exactly. There seemed to be a circle of scholarship that was feverish with "anticipation" of the new mood of manipulating nature to make her talk. These men were constantly under suspicion in those days of superstition, and circulated their unpublished manuscripts freely among themselves in order to share ideas and to inseminate one another with encouragement and experimental results.

Some names, such as Bruno's, would definitely not pass any censor in England after 1600, or in Spain, or in Italy. But there were very close relations between scholars in England and those on the Continent who searched for the knowledge of physical process, and this should be kept in mind. The courier system was used, and it seemed to work well in keeping open the channels of communication between the men who searched for the procedures that would unlock the laws of physical process. As noted earlier in this volume, Bacon collected all the works he could possibly obtain, and it took much corresponding and much money for scribes and couriers and supplies.

The wrestling of power from the earth was in fashion, and the race was on to see who could come up with the proper procedures for doing it in the best and fastest ways. The New World was being gutted and raped of all the raw material the ships could carry, and the trade with the East was at an all-time peak. This was the age of the mercantile giant, and the various nations were all bursting with the enterprise of a better and different life for its people and its men of personal power and skills. The schools were full of the discontented scholars who would attend any and all talks where the scholastic method and the scholastic Aristotle were being roasted by a commentator who was one of the new breed of men. Bacon saw the new approach to national welfare as being one of owning the technical know-how and being able to produce the material things needed to raise the general welfare of the nation and its position of prestige on the international stage. The center of that stage was shifting from the Mediterranean to the Atlantic, and the time for decisive action was *now*.

After James became king and spent considerable time in Scotland on extended holidays, during which he took the court with him, Bacon took over the reigns and received ambassadors and scholars from all over the world at Whitehall. Bacon had seen Europe as a young man and wanted to have in England a court that could keep pace with the others. Bacon wanted to remain a part of the western coalition, even if it entailed a working tolerance for Romanism (as long as the relationship was "sans politique"). Bacon's relationship with Tobie, who was very close to Bellarmine, demonstrates this. Bacon makes no bones about his desire that his work be acceptable to Roman theologians. With the defeat of Philip and the defeat of Tyrone, the urgency of English autonomy had passed. James did not have the same challenge that Elizabeth had had, and Bacon adapted his aim to suit the new mood. That mood was one of integration as a full-fledged Catholic member of a Christian League of the west. James had no great identification with the English nation. His reign was over Great Brittany. The aim of Bacon, who was completely identified with a sovereign England, was to re-establish the sovereignty of England as new technical power, the cradle of knowledge in the west. This was never taken seriously by James.

The state in Bacon's day was loaded with intrigue and opposing factions. It was a nightmare of hidden deals and counter-deals. From experience, Bacon knew that an act could be taken out of context and made to look like any vice or virtue those analyzing it wanted it to be. In putting the emphasis on the nature of the offerer in order to ascertain the nature of the tribute, Bacon is being very astute. His point is that these virtues are highly relative to the intricate motives of political intrigue.

I doubt that Bacon thought he was without integrity just because his enemies said he took a bribe. When he said that he was guilty, I believe what he meant was that he was then aware of *why the tribute to the office was made*. In short, he was saying that it is the briber who had defined the act, and that he had indeed accepted the tribute. If one studies Bacon very thoroughly there is no way in which one could hold that Bacon owned anything at all. Nothing was really his own. All that he had was instrumental monies and housing and lands in order that he might be able to operate politically within the court. He paid out much more than he had, in order to collect the items of knowledge for his encyclopedia of knowledge for England. Bacon played a dangerous game, and in the end his enemies got the drop on him. That is about the only way to describe the affair with candor and accuracy.

Human occasions were the result of the coincidence of human power and human will. Therefore the victory for a man was to have his will and power in complete harmony with the will and power of nature and with the teachings of the state on morality. A man's mind, says Bacon, should be concentric with the will of Providence. Here we see Bacon very much in tune with the themes of his time: the duality of the human mind and the dual nature of Providence as natural and societal.

Insofar as a man was following Providence, he was prudent in society and pragmatic in his science of nature. Bacon was impatient with the idea of inquiry for its own sake; and, in keeping with the philosophers of nature, he wrote that the use of knowledge was for material and human power in order that men could raise themselves to their rightful place "over" the rest of nature. Here Bacon is a Christian and must talk about "over nature." The libertine philosophers of nature would say "in nature." In his *Essays,* he remarks that one should study men more than one should study books, if one is to be able to handle himself in society. To understand matters is not enough; one must understand how to *remedy* matters. "Some can stack the deck of cards well but not be able to play them." One needs cunning to survive in the world. The technique of conversing is a science, a science that should be studied in order that one achieve his aims. Bacon taught that delay also played a crucial role in successful occasion. Occasions ripened, and sensitivity to this was crucial. One should be able to make a judgment on this. Observation and operation are both used, but the timing for the use of one or the other is the trick to be learned. One first observes, and then speeds to operate when the ripening sets in. This demonstrates the complete parrallelity of Bacon's theory of natural science and his theory of social science.

Again, he writes that only the middle way is the work of the many. To excel one must not make unseasonable motion; rather, he must take his time according to how the matter may progress in society. Few men know how to tell time by the matter rather than by their own impatience. Those who jump in too soon, and those who miss the clues and jump in too late, have not learned the art of successful occasion. Choosing *the* time critically is to save time. Here, too, is the parallel of his scientific method, applied to the science of social occasion.

Youth or extreme age are both in themselves not fortunate for proper counsel. The two of them together is best. Here as usual Bacon uses the popular theme of his time, the coincidence of contraries. Again, he uses the parallel of his theory of knowledge. Occasion of counsel is a complicated affair. Both groups of men and individual men should be used. One places trust, and sometimes there is not loyalty there. There are loyal men, though, and one must choose and take a calculated risk in doing so. Choose men who are not to gain in the situation if it is a matter of the public trust. A counselor should be skilled in the matters, and not necessarily in knowledge of the person who uses him. But the man who uses the counseling should be skilled in knowing the man he asks for help.

A long table is a poor occasion "because the men at the upper end will sway the business." Business is best achieved if one keeps in mind that old men are actors and young men are too altruistic. Bacon records in his *Essays* also that he has noted that "young men can be old in hours if they lose no time," and that the youth is good in business matters. Actually, Bacon says a family and children are a great impediment to a man. He also notices that the situation wherein "posterity is in the care of those with no posterity," has been the custom. Perpetuation through physical generation is for beasts. Man perpetuates best his unique kind by "memory, merit and noble work." Bacon notes that "churchmen will not water the ground if they first must fill a pool." In short, man cannot care for his fellow man if he has a family to care for, since they will have to come first. Women and children are "the discipline of humanity." An older man should never marry, and a young man should always put it off. Single men make good inquisitors because they have not been tempered by the experience of family life.

Freedom of speech can be turned into freedom of thought. Fair retreat or even submission can yield good knowledge of the other person's mind. As the Spaniards say, "Tell a lie and find out a truth." For public occasions openness is best, but in private matters secrecy is preferable. Bacon here sees man in a dual role in society. Man as social being should relate to the public side of his reality in an open way. But considered as an individual, man is autonomous in the service of his own survival. As an individual, man is entitled to privacy. Everything is seasonal. One must use human emotions as nature uses her moods. One should produce that setting which meets the nature of that situation, just as nature provides the proper setting to meet the requirements of the nature of her season. Love alone cannot bring on occasions of merit and spirit. Great men do not get mixed up with love. One cannot love and maintain his wisdom. It is best to diffuse this secret inclination that all men have. It then produces occasions of greater worth.

Great place has its trials. Men with great responsibility "are servants three times." They are servants to the sovereign, to the state, and to fame. When one seeks power over others, he loses power over himself. One who has power has lost freedom. It is a painful business to rise in the state, and it gets more and more painful as one achieves more and more responsibility. It is a base thing to submit to indignity, but one gains dignity in this way many times. "The stand is slippery and the fall is inevitable." What is really sad is that a man in a high place dies well known to all and not known at all to himself. If one seeks power, it should be to do good for others. Bacon sees no other use for power. If one is to do good for others he must have power and lots of it. "Good thoughts are no better than good dreams if they not be put into good acts."

In order to know how to do good for others with power, one should imitate those in the past insofar as they have succeeded in serving humanity. Those of bygone days who have withstood the test of time and upon examination are seen to have left good results should be imitated. "Examples imitated are a globe of percepts." Here Bacon uses the popular style of the macro-micro theme of the day. The globe is the particular head of a person, and this rational globe is a microcosm of the macrocosm, the rational universe. This is in the Philonic tradition. Bacon says that new-comers should also be watched and imitated. Nothing that works well should be left unnoticed by statesmen. The new and the old have equal worth. As in Bruno, the challenge is to diagnose one's need correctly and use the proper remedy. It all boils down to judgment. This holds true in social science as well as in natural science.

What is sought is the proper action to meet the proper need. The proper need is the welfare of the people and the state, but this is difficult to discern, because these appear to be contraries. *One must be wise enough to discern their latent structures, so that one can discover a common law which will be the coincidence of them.* Learned governance, whether by a monarch or by an individual learning self-control, gains the insight that contrary needs can be brought into a coincidental state. Here one sees the theme of Bruno's *Heroic Frenzies* and the *Spaccio*.

One in power should not give out with surprises. If he finds that he must detour from the customary path, he should explain every move he makes. Authority has its vices. They are delay, corruption, roughness, and expediency. The use of severity may be necessary, but at worst brings with it a fear, a fear authority might need. However, this use of severity should be temporary, and the people should be relieved of it as soon as the emergency has passed. Roughness, however, breeds hate and should be avoided. Men in authority should exercise their authority calmly. They should assume their right as an accepted fact and then voice it with claim and challenge. One should never give to the person the respect due the office. "Rising is like a winding staircase, wide in the climb and well balanced."

After one has reached high place he should be tender to those he has left behind in the climb. These men are now not his competitors and should be treated as the men they now are. Bribery should be discouraged. "Do not bind thy own hands or the hands of thy servants from taking but bind the hand of the offerer." These words of Bacon's hold that integrity is something to be learned rather than habit which can be enforced! Integrity in use was the coincidence of integrity professed and integrity made manifest. As in all virtues which were seen as complicated things (just as were the objects of study in natural science), integrity had latent laws which must be drawn out from close observation of integrity manifest and integrity professed. One could compare the claim to integrity by a man with the factual record of his manifest actions and thereby make a judgment about his use of this tool for political expediency.

I think that Bacon, like Bruno, understood virtues as relative, and that it is almost impossible to judge an act unless one uses a human utilitarian definition of the virtue. The ultimate values are never lost sight of, in Bruno. In Bacon, the radical results are all that counts. The welfare of the state as a good, both for the entire collective and for the head of state, is the true goal. This goal can and must be attained, and the use of the virtues is not a simple matter. From a practical frame of reference, when is tribute to an office to be diagnosed as bribery? Bacon felt that the clue came in the nature of the offerer. From a good man a tribute to the office might be simply that. From a man with well-balanced judgment the tribute might be a means of harmonizing divergent offices by lessening the losses of one office through yielding some goods to that office which may insure its stability. I think Bacon meant that the act cannot be judged as a naked thing. It is only the "explicatio," and one would have to know the "implicatio" (its latent cause) and its "complicatio" (its nature or tie-in with the welfare of the state).

For occasions of civil matters, boldness was important to Bacon. And yet, "boldness is the child of ignorance." One must admit, though, that as a civil device it keeps both the weak and the strong in line. "Natural body has its montebanks and so has the body politic." In order to be a good executive one needs to be able to ignore danger. In matters of commanding, though, this boldness is not such an asset.

In civil matters ancient nobility is the "act of time" and new nobility is the "act of power." A state must be balanced. Too much nobility is a drain on the seat of government and on the people. The top-heavy state will be paralyzed with poverty. The state would die in anarchy if put into the people's hands. Therefore, there ought to be just enough nobility to keep the unfit in tow. Insolence in the common people is good neither for them nor for the state. The victory is in winning their wills, and this is done by *legitimate nobility,* which can be *either ancient or new.*

Among the people there are bonds deeper than the state, which follow the law of reason only. Therefore the state must also win the hearts of the people as much as is necessary to withstand hatred of the state. If dislike of the state sets in, it may be best simply to ignore it, and it will wear down. Severe force may only make it worse. Again *correct diagnosis* is important. Forced obedience is not good. It is willing assent which makes a state powerful. "Great persons in the state should be as the primum mobile of the planets, keeping the planets swift in their highest motions and keeping the planets moving softly in their own orbs." Bacon here holds the theory that the leaders in government should inspire immediate and spontaneous obedience around the throne as if the welfare of the throne is not understood apart from the welfare of each and every man. This view of the state as collected subject tacitly entails a Stoic enjoyment of one's role as subject. One becomes integral to the state, and the state becomes integral to one's welfare. Here again, is the footprint of Philo Judea.

Especially interesting is the model of every man as a planet or a world. This was a favorite Brunian image, from Philo Judea. For Bruno, each man was a world, and the microcosms were integrated into the infinity of these micro-worlds, or the macro-world. The state was a macro-world for the subject. The state was a micro-world when one contemplated the universe of states, the macro-world of humanity. This Brunian notion runs all through Bacon's work. It is understandable that Bacon could not mention Bruno by name in those days.

Bacon notes that "Suffering has its limits but fear is without end." Therefore, people can take some suffering, and they will forget it after the trial is over; but when people become afraid, then these fears are very hard to dispell. Even after the cause of fear is removed, the fear will still linger. "The cord will break at the last by the weakest pull". Therefore, there should be as much openness in public matters as possible, and all severity should be completely understood by the general public. This entails that severity is legitimate for the safeguarding of the state, and is therefore in each man's interest.

Bacon quotes Cosimo de Medici of Florence and reminds his reader that Cosimo had taught that it was given by commandment that one should forgive his enemies, but that the commandment did not say anything about forgiving one's friends. Bacon says that the discovery that a man must love himself better than he can love another should not be upsetting. It should, however, be understood that revenge is rejection of the laws of the state, and that one cannot give penalty where the state does not. Repentance on the part of one's friends may be obtained by bringing the matter to his attention. Otherwise, the matter is best taken in stride. Wounds should not be kept green. One should husband the hour, and let the past be the past. However, if public revenge is available to one he could handle the matter in that way.

Bacon uses the term "heroic virtue." He says that this is fortitude when it is moral courage in the face of adversity. Adversity has its value as that which generates moral fortitude. Prosperity is useful because it can generate temperance. "Virtue is like precious odors. It is more fragrant when crushed." He holds that prosperity put to the test discovers vice, and that adversity put to the test will outline virtue. Bacon notes that sometimes there is undue obscurity in the state due to treating small matters as one should treat great matters. Those who are not good politicians make this error. In order to lead the opposition astray in great matters, one should mislead them in order to be able to surprise them. But this is a technique that is to be used appropriately by men in the right situation.

Secrecy in morals and in politics is useful. In grave matters one cannot allow the face to betray all the plans. At Trent, the Schoolmen were like the astronomers who had feigned eccentrics and epicycles and engines of orbs to save the phenomena (according to them). All the time they knew that there were no such things. These astronomers were simply out to save their practices. The Schoolmen were doing the same thing at Trent. They were all explaining the divine as human and excusing this as good intentions. Bacon echoes Bruno when he writes: "It adds deformity to the ape to make it so like a man". Religion is deformed by making it so like superstition. Good laws are corrupted into a number of petty observances, which are tied to superstitions. "Superstition without a veil is a deformed thing."

Here Bacon seems to claim that if superstition is used to create useful audio-visual aids in the service of good laws, then this superstition should be much better controlled, so that it remains credible. In this time Bacon felt that it had gotten out of hand, insofar as it was not controlled and parcelled out with expertise. The "crazy astronomers" and the "Schoolmen at Trent" were no longer able to hide their webs behind their faces. Bruno had also made this criticism of mathematics in science and syllogisticism in argument. Men had allowed themselves to fall in love with their tools, Bruno wrote (see *Infinite Worlds*).

3.

LEGITIMATE INTERPRETATION

BACON REPEATS Bruno's criticism of scholars who confuse their mathematics or their models with natural objects. Bruno wrote a book on this confused use of theoretical entities and theoretical models. Bruno also writes that there is absolutely no reason at all to accept these fantastic motors when we do not need to. Bruno also writes about the confusion of metaphor with fact in religious doctrine, which turned natural religion into gross superstition. But Bruno did not reject the theoretical models in astronomy on the same grounds that Bacon did.

Bruno understood the theoretical model and the theoretical entity, but he insisted that the "presupposto" must be kept as simple as possible. Here Bruno understood that the universe demonstrated universal law-like regularity in its process and a unity in the complete relatedness of all natural bodies; he wrote many hypotheses which were much simpler than the old ones. Bruno cautioned that the planets were natural bodies, just like any body on earth, and would not orbit in a perfect circle. Bruno cautioned that the sun was only another star, and that an infinite number of solar systems had their own suns.

Bruno was completely at home with theoretical models and theoretical entities—so long as the scientist did not confuse them with the elusive natural process which he projected them into, in order to capture an insight into more of the elusive laws of cosmic operation. Bacon, however, threw the baby out with the bath water when he made no distinction between the metaphorical angels and saints of religion and the epicycles and orbits of the astronomer.

Bacon's journals were based squarely on the metaphysics of the philosophers of nature in his own time and did not go as far as some of them. Indeed, in his fear of superstition and dogma which was without reason, Bacon was held back in his appreciation of the role of mathematics in theoretical natural philosophy.

Bacon's latent forms and configurations had to be explicated from physical objects taken as complicated objects, just as in Cusa. For Bacon, the implicatory nature of a physical object was to be co-incidental with the explicated, sensual, physical form of it. But both the latent nature of the *co-incident* and of the implicatory features of physical objects could only be understood in Bacon through laborious *comparative enumeration* and classification of the explicated physical sensual form. Bacon's search for the general logic as to exactly how one should attain the latent forms and latent configurations through manipulation of the physical was doomed to failure *by his rejection of the calculated risk* upon which all theoretical natural science is based. In fairness to Bacon, though, *he rejected simple enumeration* as puerile.

Bacon did not understand the element of deductive speculation in all inductive physical science procedure. It is there, from the perception of physical bodies to the mathematical symbolization of the theoretical entity. The intuition of exactly this deductive-speculative element in the physical process accompanies mathematics and enables theoretical men of science to lay down ever new complementary laws of nature. Bacon did not see it because he was not a metaphysician, a physicist, a mathematician, an engineer, a chemist, or a medical doctor who understood the *theoretical foundations* of natural philosophy as being admittedly locked up in the physically perceived object. Bacon did not realize that what he called the "laws of nature" were creations of the human mind. Bruno, on the other hand, understood this well.

Bacon could not allow human thought "the free creation" because he was a victim of *the times* (as he so often pointed out to us in his writings). I do not think anyone need apologize for Bacon. Nor should Bacon apologize for himself. Bruno was burned alive for not "turning freedom of speaking (and writing) into freedom of thought," and Vanini received the same treatment as late as 1619! Why should Bacon desire that treatment? Besides, Bacon held down a tough political job, and he was instrumental in the actual affairs of state in England. He wanted to continue in his place. He was *doing* important things.

Nicholas of Cusa had written that reality had a dual nature. On the one hand, there was the physical world of physical natures, and on the other hand there was the contrary of this physical world of physical things, which was its intelligible structure. This was a Platonic model. But Cusanus christianized this model. He writes that these two contraries fold up or co-incide in God. God is the *complicatio*, the world of physical nature is the *explicatio*, and the intelligible structure of the physical world is the *implicatio*. Nicholas of Cusa wrote that God could not be known. Only the physical world could be known, once in a naïve way through the senses and again in an intelligible way through the understanding. Conjecture or hypothesis was the vehicle used to attempt to correlate the physical processes of the common senses with the intelligible processes of the understanding. These conjectures would be based upon reasoning, which is comparing. The language of comparison is mathematical, as in Plato.

For Cusa, the more that we fathom of this implicatory world of the understanding, the more aware we become of the fact that there is an *indeterminate potential field of implication* lying ahead of us. Therefore the physical world is indeterminate. Thus, writes Cusanus, "knowledge is learned ignorance." Cusanus taught that physical things must be compared with each other, in order that their composition be elucidated through the correlation of the explicated object (the existential thing) and the implicated object (the intelligible object). This correlation will be a recipe and will be written in the language of precise proportions, mathematics. With these recipes man can understand the mundane world around him and can appropriate the mundane powers to his own use for a better appreciation of God's omnipotency.

Bruno then came along and materialized this doctrine of the co-incidence of contraries. The infinite and the finite never coincided in Cusanus. The indeterminate and the finite coincided (the implicatory and explicatory) in the precision of mathematics. The Infinite was not comparable to anything, in Cusanus. The Absolute Infinite and the Absolute Limit were not contraries; they were both God. Human intelligences mistakenly tried to know God analytically and mistakenly put their sensually generalized human notion of finite on a par with the purely intellectual vision of God, as the greatest finite. The finite was a sensually generated notion, and its contrary must be the indeterminate *of the same species,* which would be a generalization about the physical from mathematical reasoning. Therefore, these two notions could coincide in the notion of an infinite mathematical series. However, this infinite would not be revealing of the structural human intellect as its own unique identity, the creation of an Unknowable (God). This infinite would be a number tied to physical things.

When we say Absolute Limit as pertaining to God, we mean that God is present anywhere simultaneously. When we say Absolute *Infinite* as pertaining to God, we mean that God is everywhere and nowhere. Therefore, we must distinguish between these two kinds of notions—one kind of notion that is from human experience as creature experience, and the other kind of notion that is from man as the creation of an Unknowable God and made in the image of that God. The Absolute Infinite and the Absolute Limit, the Absolute Maximum and the Absolute Minimum, are Unknowable and Incomprehensible. Cusanus says that when we do philosophy we should deal with the species of notions from human experience rather than try to deal with theological notions. Therefore in natural philosophy we will deal with the indeterminate and the finite, and in mathematics we can deal with the infinite and the finite as *we reason by analogy* from the physical world of experience.

Cusa held that the theological notion of God as All-Knowing cannot be expressed in natural philosophy from the generalization of physical experience. The philosophical notion, therefore, is Nature. Let us, in philosophy, distinguish between the Absolute Maximum (God) and Nature. All-Knowing entails the full range from the least to the most. Therefore, let us know that the term Absolute Minimum (God) is distinguished from the philosophical term, Minimum (Nature).

In order to understand our obscure philosophical thought structures, we must start in the world of physical things, and by reasoning about (comparing) physical things we may be able to find lucid, intelligible contents that can make our obscure thought structures visible to us. This can only be done by increasing our ignorance. The more we realize exactly what eludes us, the more we can precisely design our material inquiry to embody those obscure human thought structures that elude us.

Bruno materialized the metaphysics of Cusanus. The Absolutes were taken as having a value only for moral teachings. These absolutes were seen as traditional definitions, written by men who were the moral leaders. For Bruno, only those leaders who did not violate the welfare of "whole men" were to be respected. Society for Bruno must be well balanced; as in Plato, the society must harmonize all the human powers. Bruno also materialized Cusanus in his theory of knowledge. God, the *complicatio,* was the essential ratio in all things. Each thing had a dual nature, its explicated side in the physical world, and its implicatory side that was intelligible. Like da Vinci, who pulled from Cusanus, Bruno describes the world of physical nature as an intelligible masterpiece. From the Stoics is retained the idea that the world is rational. So, for Bruno, the world is a rational organism spun from the sensible and intelligible powers of human beings *out of a concrete cosmos.* That is, an energetic, non-corporeal, natural material process that eluded the common senses of men, although it collided with the irritability of these senses and thus produced sensation in man's sensibility. The law and order of individual human structure did the rest, with the conditioning of culture. Culture was a macro-man which controlled the micro-man.

Bacon adopted all of this. It was the most serious philosophy of the times, although never directly quoted. Bruno and some other philosophers of nature could not *at that time* be reconciled with orthodox religion. Bacon had to trim these teachings to fit the rigid orthodoxy of the English Catholic church. Remember, Nicholas of Cusa was a Cardinal in the Roman Catholic Church. His name would not, at this time, have been held up for full appreciation in England, due to the religious problems of the day. So, Bacon hired a court of scribes and thinkers to help him to put all of the best of these teachings into English form. *This* is his contribution, and it is an important one. But a nation of about two million people, desperate for political survival and religious autonomy, needed knowledge of practical technology over nature. Therefore, in natural philosophy Cusa's and Bruno's views were acceptable, but *their names were not acceptable.*

The "minimum" was a physical object, which Bacon understood to have a compound nature. This compound nature had to be broken down into categories of physical characteristics. A minimum number of "like" and "unlike" characteristics had to be established for inclusion of a physical object in a descriptive category. Each descriptive category—for example, heat—through its range of characteristics was further manipulated physically to make manifest the latent process and latent configurations of the phenomenon. In this way, particular effects could be described for each object. These particular effects (for each compound nature) should be exercised to ascertain a maximum and minimum performance for them in *contrived* physical situations, aimed at utility. Now, as efficient causes, these effects are defined (through their minimum-to-maximum range) as composing a structural composition of the physical object or phenomenon. This structural composition must be broken down into its particles or simple forms. Habits of nature can be traced through the compound natures to the simple natures.

Essential characteristics of a body composed its simple nature. Formal causes of these efficient causes were universal laws of nature imbedded in the physically perceived event/object. Middle axioms could be made about the *structural compositions*. These middle axioms could yield the particles and their simple connectedness. Taking the structural composition as minimum, one could establish a descriptive range of a minimum—a maximum number of various simple particles. From this range one could define materials involved. The material formula elicited through this study of a minimum number of simple materials and a maximum number of simple materials would be the highest cause to be understood—the material cause. It would also be the most elusive.

Bacon did not completely understand the metaphysics of Cusanus and Bruno. Bacon wanted only to deal with the *practical* parts of natural philosophy: the efficient causes and physical substances. The theoretical parts of natural philosophy (the formal and material causes) were best described as those universal laws of nature which constituted for Bacon the *physical* forms in which matter was perceived. These formal causes were limited by and created out of the middle axioms of human thought, which were *barely* more than the physical experiences which formed them. Forms expressed physical nature, unique physical forms containing "given" physical natures. Physical particles and physical structure were what constituted latent process and latent configurations.

For Bacon, "latent" meant obscured by lack of technology, or skill, or senses. The latent became harnessed as physical power, due to persistent *physical* manipulations of compound natures in order that one can "break up" that compound nature into its simpler natures or nature. In this way, one could best appropriate these simple natures into more *useful* arrangements. Here, Bacon is influenced by Galileo. The logic of the coincidence of contraries demonstrated that any physical characteristic of natural power could be understood only in comparison to some other physical characteristic of valued power. "To think is to compare," said Cusanus. Therefore, there were to be *three* logical positions in any physical event/object under study. *The* minimum or *the* maximum, *a* maximum, and *a* minimum. *The* minimum or *the* maximum would be of *composite* nature; *a* logical maximum and *a* logical minimum could be brought to bear upon it comparatively. Bacon used Bruno's logic from the *De Monade*, which is Cusan.

All the neo-Platonists, such as Cusa, da Vinci, Bruno, and Galileo, taught that relative measurement of relative characteristics made upon relative bodies created a contingent world—one based squarely on logical perspectives of reasonable measurement. This rationale held for the social life in political theories of the day, but it was cloaked by a Scriptural exegesis. This in no way obliterated the mandate of the world of appearances for social theory. Nor did it provide primacy to either the logical or the physical realities. Rather, the most *real* in the metaphysics of the coincidence of contraries is the *human* real, which is the human *synthesis* of the human intellectual forms with the human physical forms accomplished by the human reason (Bruno and Cusa). Reason must be understood here as the composite of the intellectual and the physical. Reason is the human *complicatio,* which can be analytically reduced to the *implicatio* and the *explicatio.* The universal *explicatio* is the common world of physical appearances for all men in life. The universal *implicatio* is the common theoretical world of intellectual objects for all men of positive science. They coincide in the unity of nature for the common senses and the unity, God, for the intellect. The universal *explicatio* is communicated through the language of fact. The universal *implicatio* is communicated through the language of theoretical science. The principle of implication provides the laws for explication, and this is the science of the *complicatio,* the human world as creation of God.

The early modern metaphysics of the macrocosm-microcosm model, based upon Cusanus' coincidence of contraries, marks a transition to the synthesis of the common senses with the intellect. These faculties coincide in man and his reasonable activity; reality will now be captured by human *reason,* seen as the coincidence of the contraries of common sense and common intellect. Positive theoretical science can result from the common intellect, and a common world of existential objects can be verified by the common sense. These two universal kinds of knowledge will be in harmony with each other through the adjustments made by the common reason. The language of reason will explain the common sense world through the common intellectual forms that are perfected through the pragmatic demonstration of the physical world.

There are *two* infinitely large sets of objects, one infinitely large physically and the other infinitely large theoretically. These two infinitely large worlds are brought together through two infinitely small sets of objects, one infinitely small physical set, and one infinitely small theoretical set. *This was the theoretical position which was causing much comment in Bacon's day.*

Bacon collected all the notes on this he could get, and used them as well as he could to make it appear that their value would serve the nation. In the face of overwhelming odds (I think that Bacon's downfall was the result), Bacon wrote, in the same vein as Bruno, that "Truth is the daughter of Time and not the daughter of authority." This indicates a deep and abiding confidence in the rational evolution of the human species, which would be restrained permanently by no authority whatsoever. Very often, Bacon says that he would rather tolerate all religions in all countries and not force anyone to worship God only in the one ritual. He did write that within the boundaries of each state the domestic peace would hinge on a harmony of opinions about the political authority in that state. He also added that to rule beasts is no victory at all, and that the truly noble man would be able to lead men through the love he would inspire in them for his leadership.

It is easy to lose the flavor of Bacon's days, and it takes a great deal of unbiased reading to understand the atmosphere in which he lived. When one has read widely, on both sides of the old biases on this period, one must read rather widely in all the disciplines for this period of time. Finally there begins to emerge a pretty sound reproduction of those days and the men who lived through them. Bacon, when studied within his own times, emerges as a political engineer of the first rank. His journals emerge in the encyclopedic style which has been popular since the last years of the fifteenth century. These journals attempted to gather all the knowledge mankind had stumbled upon. There were manuscripts copied by scribes *who took a little bit of this and a little bit of that* under Bacon's editorial supervision. These works had to be fitted into the times in order for them to survive.

What was the fate of these days? Were they a doomsday, or a brave new world? The new mathematics and the new mechanics, together with the realization that the heavens changed and were corruptible, brought with them an unfortunate literature among the writers and pessimists who were looking for new evidence with which to support their power and their conservative practices. The star of 1572 and the star of 1604 had given the philosophers of nature more insight into the one-world cosmos of Plato, rather than the two-world cosmos of Aristotle. Plato had taught that the distinction between the logical and the physical could be made, and that the physical world was then correlated with the logical world by intellectual formulas. This correlation Plato called "participation." From all the neo-Platonists through to Cusanus and Bruno, Plato's teaching brought with it a theory of the complete relativity of human reality.

As against this teaching, the Aristotelian teaching of an absolute cleavage between the changeable physical and the unchangeable celestial worlds had been instituted by the theology of the day as the correct view of reality. Around the physics of Aristotle, the Christian philosophers had also spun a web of Christian theory of knowledge and Christian natural science. This called for leaving the heavens alone. It also called for the absolute split of reality into the heavenly world and the physical world. Concepts such as "infinite" and "eternal" or "unchanging" were not to be applied to the physical world, which was seen to be a "valley of tears" and a "lower place", in which man must wallow in order to purify himself for death. Human suffering was of great value, as it earned a man grace for the journey to Heaven.

For Bruno this was not the way things really were. Religion was a system of symbols, used to control masses of people. Religion at this time was the institution that fastened man's eyes and ears to the ground and taught him that to look into the heavens as he would look into the forest, would be a sin. Bruno taught that this was *not* so. The sky and its lights were just more natural phenomena, and they were made of the same elements as the bodies on earth. There was one human universe for Bruno, and the only meaningful distinction to be made was the one which the early Greeks had made, especially Plato; this was the distinction between the world of common sense and the world of the intellect. This was the distinction between the visible for man and the invisible for man's gross observation. The invisible was material but could not be sensed by human common senses, as the human perceptual apparatus was too coarse. However, man could refine his common sense information through analysis and mathematical reasoning, and could create intellectual forms that were correlates of that material of nature which could be understood but not physically observed. What could be grasped then would be the relations between bodies and the relations between the relations between bodies. Bacon liked all this.

In Bacon's day John Donne wrote the doomsday lament and others followed suit. The universe was slipping away from man, the sinner, and soon the total corruption of the universe would be consummated, due to the refusal of men to glorify God. The literature abounded with this theme of the decaying heavens and decadent human life. Bruno wrote in a different vein. In the *Spaccio* he writes of a completely changed heaven, but it is all excellent. Jove cleans house and throws out all the false formulas that have bound the moral concepts. He replaces the false formulas with the *proper formulas* in which the moral concepts could participate, so that they would function as virtues for existential human welfare. Leisure could only stay as a pattern if she was in a co-operative relationship with work. Female virginity could only stay as a pattern in union with meaningful continence and satisfaction for existential human welfare.

In order to stay in Heaven, each virtue had to be a pattern of relatedness with fellow virtues, so that the heavenly formula if practical on earth would realize human welfare on earth. *These virtues in heaven were to be locked by definition into human welfare and human well-being on the earth.* For Bruno, the heavens were being set straight. The idea that the heavens were in flux was no surprise to him and merely proved that the universe was one organism. Man was an internal part of that organism. For Bruno, there was nothing to fear but human ignorance.

Bacon follows Bruno on this, and in his *Essays* he treats the virtues and the vices in the same way that Bruno does in the *Spaccio*. They are all relative to the situation in which a man finds himself. Actually all of this is only *the materializing of the doctrine of contraries* spelled out by Cusanus. As materialized, Cusa's dialectic reads: things or concepts are *complicatio,* and they may in one situation exhibit one meaning (*explicatio*) and in another situation exhibit another meaning (*implicatio*). For each *"explicatio"* has its contrary *implicatio,* and the *explicatio* and the *implicatio* co-incide in the *complicatio.*

There is no doubt that Bacon realized that a moral ideology was needed as an integral part of a political system. There is no doubt that he demonstrated in his behavior over a long period of time that in his day and age Christianity was the ideology that was in vogue and had to be used. He frankly calls his collections and his *Essays* "a birth of time and not of wit". I take this to mean that, as he said in the *Advancement,* there was much more he could say of his wit, but he would not do so at that time. Rather, he would base his insights upon the ancient ways. This is what he did in his *Essays.*

Bacon wrote that innovations at first may appear misshapen. Their strangeness, he contends, makes them more of a curiosity than a thing of usefulness. This means, for example, that any moral ideology introduced as an alternative to the Christianity (then in vogue) would be too much of a curiosity to be useful or effective. Conformity can be just as troublesome as change, because time does not stand still, and will, therefore, bring forth its newborn in spite of custom. Time itself, though, operates so profoundly and efficiently in producing its offspring that it operates quietly and by scarcely perceptible degrees. "Time" itself, then, is no problem; it is the "times" that obstruct human realization.

Bacon writes that men with innovations should follow this example which "time" has given us, and should innovate just as quietly and just as imperceptibly. States or nations cannot support the unexpected, Bacon says. And he adds that the new is unlooked-for. This reminds one of Bruno, who writes, "We only look for the fruits of the trees which we ourselves plant." One should not experiment with states or nations in Bacon's day. He cautioned that the reformation may result from mere love of change, if the reformation is not useful, and does not carry what is needed by the state. A reformation based upon mere love of change, rather than upon what is urgently needed and useful to the state, may well lead to merely more love of change. It is better to "stand upon the ancient way and then look about us and discover what is the straight and right way, and so to walk it," Bacon suggests. He goes on to say that in government we should "hold the novelty suspect".

Here Bacon points out the contrary nature of innovation: it is strange, but it could be useful. In one place he writes, "no new remedies, no new cures." He tells us to stand with the Ancient way. In other places, he has denounced undue fixation on the ancients. He has also told us to find ancient examples, "the best and the fittest", to emulate. Bacon seems to be saying here, as he does all through his writings, that all things are relative to judging the appropriate or most prudent move to make. If one simultaneously imitates nature and time, one will be sensitive to the mood of the nation, because time carries prudential truth. Somehow, one feels that Bacon soundly realizes that the human scene will evolute as human knowledge increases. Human readiness for more and more of nature's possibilities will evolve, as every man becomes more and more empowered to harness and appropriate to his own increased welfare more and more of the natural creatures and inanimate natures around him. It almost seems inevitable to Bacon that the "nobles" among the human race will lead the way to human control over nature, which is the rightful claim of able men.

The success of this leadership will hinge upon the learned governor. The learned governor will be a whole man. This "whole man" will hold above all else the hearts of the people, and wield the sword of the King of kings. This will entail the proper balance of the Myth and the Truth. This will entail the proper balance of the new and the old. This will entail the proper balance of reward and punishment, as the learned governor assumes the task of being "god to man."

Bacon writes in his *Essays* that the learned governor should have contact with the secretaries or scribes in all lands. In this way, one can know what knowledge has been found, and who has it, and what is to be done with it. Bacon frankly suggests "one should keep the thoughts but not their dress." For Bacon, one should accentuate likenesses between foreign customs, as well as maintain one's integrity, to facilitate intercourse between secretaries. This also alludes to the need to tailor natural scientific findings to national needs before teaching them at home.

Bacon writes that "It is one thing to mingle contraries and another thing to interchange them." A monarch cannot "command an end without enduring the means." Leadership can be destroyed if it institutes an inappropriate interchanging of power by pressing too hard and relaxing too much. Timing is of the essence in using power. Danger is danger, and must be recognized correctly. Neighboring countries must be marked closely as to their growth and their interests. A ruler is both a god and a man to his own secondary nobility. As a god, the ruler bridles their will, and as a man he should bridle their power. A ruler must know what he can achieve successfully and what he is not ready to achieve as yet. After all, the only direction left to a Monarch is down; Bacon writes that "kings have little desire and much to fear." The country must be kept balanced in social classes and in ports of trade.

Overgrown nobility and overgrown theologians are a problem. The population is not maintained by them, they live off the population. Scholars, also, must not become too many, and too much of a drain on the people. Usury is to be licensed and controlled at five percent. It should not be stopped, because it does keep money moving and enterprises emerging. "Money is like good muck, it is not good (useful) unless it is well spread." A monarch must first and foremost have the good will of the people. Hope must be alive and diffused throughout the nation. The common people must hear good speeches from the throne, and these should be frequently given, for they "fly like darts" through the kingdom and keep up hope. The throne should feed hope to every faction in the country. The throne should also divide any malcontents, and should have the military nip dangerous factions in the bud, but the military must be integrated with all other administrative agencies of the throne.

Bacon writes in his *Essays* that he would adopt another reformed religion rather than to have no religion at all. Atheism is unthinkable for him, because it is impossible to have the "belief that this universal frame is without a mind." When secondary causes are discovered, and the way in which they are linked to each other is apprehended, the laws of nature are understood. This impresses one with the mind of the universal frame. The idea of infinite seeds is not atheistic. The idea of the fourth and fifth elements is more atheistic. Democritus, Leucippus, and Epicurus weren't atheists. Bacon writes, "There is no profanity in not believing in God, the real profanity lies in what one is obligated to believe about God." He says that it is better to hold no opinion about God, than to cast a highly unworthy opinion of God. Atheism has never disturbed states; "it sets up no monarchy in a man's head". But superstition allows the *primum mobile* to ravish the spheres of government. Atheism at least leads men towards the experiences of common sense, and from there to philosophy, and to a natural piety that supports laws and reputation. Atheists must watch themselves and assume responsibility for themselves, for they have no external monarch in their head, to give them orders.

Bacon adds that atheists may therefore be guides to a public morality. Historically, atheistic times have been good times for the civil state. The people can be full of superstition. Do wise men follow fools? Rome was an analogy, Bacon felt. He quotes Cicero, who held that a pious attitude toward providence made men act religious and wise. Bacon compares man to a dog who has a good master. Through the good master the dog is able to elevate his canine nature. Bacon says that "without the confidence in, and the protection of, a nature better than one's own, man could never attain the uplifting of his human nature." Some men gather force and a faith from this belief in God. The atheists who are really dangerous "are these hypocrites who handle holy matters without any feeling at all." They are bad priests, who divide nations, and they should be cauterized, Bacon thought.

"A contemplative atheist is rare, but when they are of this kind they seem to be more than merely atheists. They indict popular religion or superstitions and so are branded as atheists by those who are adverse to their charge," Bacon writes. Here, Bacon may be supporting Bruno, as best he can in those times.

Bacon used Bruno's materialized model of the metaphysics of Cusanus for his scientific method. But, for his model of the state, he *cloaked* his social materialism with Christianity. In order to avoid what they considered to be unfortunate Roman superstitions, the English exegesis returned to a much earlier time for expertise in exegesis. The Philonic exegesis seems to have influenced Deism. Philo held that social laws are in harmony with the natural laws. The *logos* in nature was implanted there by the Creator after he had created the world. The Lord reveals this law in some men. The Father and Master of the world was first and foremost the law-giver. He who would accept the laws of the world from the maker of the world will joyfully accept the laws of nature and live in accordance with the ordering of the universe. The human goal is to live in accord with nature. The virtuous man walks in the path of right reason, following God. Right reason is according to those laws of nature which are discovered by human reason, and does not violate human reason. God is the source and guide of virtue, which is contemplative power. The road to virtue is philosophical. Philosophy embraces logic, ethics, physics, and morals. The virtuous power in man is both physical and spiritual. The Good is triple: spirit, body, and external circumstance all in harmony. Man has duties to God and duties to his fellow man.

Philo taught that laws implanted virtues. Some men intuit the laws at their source by divine inspiration or revelation. Others who live mostly by their passions follow the laws of nature as they are understood through training and education. Noble men are those who are endowed with the goal of the contemplative study of the source of all laws, or God. Whether or not a man is noble depends *not* on the social conditions of his birth in the existential world. His nobility also depends on his inspiration from the source of all laws, God. The value of his leadership can be easily discerned. Any reasonable man can understand when it is that he is being asked to violate his own nature. The most ordinary man can understand duty to his fellow man and to God. Ordinary men will follow the leadership on this, if the leadership appeals to his reason or demonstrates clearly for his common sense the commandments of God and the needs of his fellows. Some men learn these commandments quite naturally; others learn them by habit-in-practice; anl still others by learning through reason.

The Scriptures teach that God has given man the heritage of the kingdom for his use. Man will build his rightful dominion over nature with the guidance from the divine law of God. Noble men naturally inherit the mighty nation of mankind as their toiling place. The laws for human guidance follow from the history of God's creation of the world. These laws for human guidance are in complete harmony with the laws of the created nature. God, as the lawgiver, reveals Himself through the reception of His revealed law. Prudence is service to fellow men through use of the natural laws.

Bacon, in the *Advancement of Learning* (II, xvii, 1, 2, 3, 4, 5) makes it clear that cloaked language may be necessary for the natural and civil scientist. The proper interplay of "posita juris" and "placita juris" must be effected in order to accomplish philanthropia (justice for everyman during his life on earth). God will administer justice for everyman after he dies. We should imitate God in our own earthly realm.

In the *Novum Organum*, Bacon stated that there should never be confrontation between the natural law and the social law. If the natural and the social are kept in harmony, says Bacon, the use of the discovered natural law enters into the nation quietly and serenely. He also states in the *Advancement* that scientists must work in some secrecy, and that a committee of them should decide what and how much to tell the monarch in the event that his leadership is not ready for their full findings. Bacon complained about the way in which the leaders of his times were chosen to rule. He did this sparingly, making passing mention of his disapproval. One is reminded of Bacon's admiration for Henry VII, who took the throne of England by his "noble" brain and brawn and not by his noble blood.

CHAPTER FOUR

THE AGE OF TRANSFORMATION (1400-2000)

1. Bacon's Legacy
2. Facts in History Versus Historical Facts
3. "Congenial" Research and "Congenial" Teaching

1.

BACON'S LEGACY

THE AGE OF TRANSFORMATION is ushered in with the philosophy of Cusanus. Here, we have for the first time in many decades the call for a positive theory of knowledge based on measuring and comparing physical bodies with each other in order to ascertain their essential characteristics. Here we have a negative theory of God. God is unknowable. The physical universe and its indeterminate physical process is understandable to man in human ways. The release of mathematics from the physical operations in which it was applied was a momentous occasion. *Now mathematics was seen as the legitimate transformation language* for very technical observations and control of physical processes.

The face of the earth became in these days a virtual beehive of activity. The raw given natures, as Bacon saw, were being transformed and converted to man-made natures. There was a new world dawning and it was all the synthesis of human creation from his human experience and his human intelligence. This creative activity of man in culture proceeded steadily and with dispatch all through the next six centuries. We, today, stand in the path hewn out of the woods of ignorance (as Bacon would say) by these men who faced death, imprisonment and public disgrace in order to get the job done. Technology, the Pallas of the re-formed intellect, has today begun to master us. Man, in the next thirty years or so, is faced with the challenge of ushering in the *Age of Balance*. This oncoming age of balance will harness the brain children of natural science. In this way man can assume his *human* role in nature with an ecumenical spirit which will support divergent views and divergent ethics to be embraced *in the unity of human empathy for human natures* as well as in the "sympathetic understanding" of non-human nature, which is the finest

129

hour of the natural sciences today.

Bacon asked that the mind "be made naked again in its simplicity and innocence" in order that natural science be successful.
Bruno taught that the "regolato sentimento" must be used in order
that ignorance and superstition be set aside for the "clear" ideas
of the disciplined mind. All of these insights have been realized
in the natural sciences. The same challenge looms ahead for the
human community for the social sciences. This can and will be
achieved as men slowly realize that social science must have a
heart. The "sympathetic understanding" of the frailty and infinite
power of the human organism will mandate the social axioms
which serve whole men born from the seeds of whole men, as
opposed to those social axioms which are written to serve logical
computers.

Bacon saw utility for human peace and welfare as the membrane
through which human experience must be filtered. Insofar as
human experience remained a gelatinous mess of hearsay (trial
and error, and gluttonous political bloating), it was the wanton
waste of human wit. Time was the author of truth for Bacon,
and time was a flow which particular "times" obstructed. But he
pointed out that "that which brings knowledge never really fails,"
although he knew that many times it had passed for almost dead,
under some authorities. Bacon, in his times, recommended that
human genius should synchronize the dialysis of human power,
with a shrewd sensitivity to the preparedness of the existential
realities. His encyclopedic labors, reflective comments, and practical synthesis of all the ideas he selected as worthy were all *a
serious attempt* to prepare a wide readership *for the dawn of a
new age.*

This age of transformation was already upon his times, and
Bacon tried to introduce "a new intellectual operation" which
would integrate invented physical scientific forms with lagging
political habits. *Legitimate method in science* would control superstition and forestall accidental intuitions from creating supernatural monsters out of those "dabblers" who would form cults
of magic. Scientific method would be torn from the dark rooms
of cloisters or magnificent private castles.

Scientific method would be based upon social law and order and a sure and steady respectability. Re-formed method of tradition called for the head of state to be the commander-in-chief over all the natural forces in the human kingdom. The natural philosopher would be this ruler's scientific brains. The technicians would run the ruler's knowledge factory. The ruler who could be "god to man on earth" would control an empire.

As commander-in-chief over all the natural resources in the empire, the head of state would depend upon these executive helpers. Part of the challenge these scientists would face entailed the close study of their learned governor. In this way, these re-formed scientists would correctly "time" their findings. Therefore, men of great theoretical insights that were born of legitimate method should either prepare the ruler and the state for change, or else remain loyal and silent and wait. Time was on their side. Knowledge is only power *if it can imitate nature* and *silently bear its fruit* for the human race. Undue slaughter of human life, inaugurated by fear of science, only made matters worse. Bacon's version of what might be a useful political plan should carry a good deal of weight, because he had actual experience in the front line of action and a desire to be knowledgeable about what he was doing.

Bacon emerges as a political engineer because his effort was to provide a blueprint for a successful nation which could accommodate the dramatic changes which were taking place all around him. There were other attempts. However, Bacon's attempts to engineer the politics of nation were needed because England was trying to operate autonomously, apart from the habits of the other Western countries at that time. England's monarch had been excommunicated from the established religion of the day. The people of England were new at this, and did not know which should come first, religion or nation. England was very much on trial, a little nation of probably two million inhabitants, surrounded by hostile neighbors (Scotland, Ireland, Rome, France, and Spain were all hostile to the new secular monarchy).

Bacon decided early in the game that autonomy of the English nation hinged upon a utilitarian use of all natural resources. The general populace was considered as natural resource to the nation and was to be husbanded properly. This entailed socializing human intelligence and human will. Bacon did not use the armchair approach himself. But he did want any light which that approach might have thrown on the science of statecraft, and he studied all theories. Bacon came to see national independence and techno-logical know-how as inseparable. The challenge was to come up with a political blueprint for change.

Philanthropia in the ancient Greek language had meant giving help to those in need. It was the twin to the word "piety." Piety and philanthropia *together* meant holiness to god and justice to men. To signal the elevated position of the human species, the word "humanity" or *humanitas* was used in the early Latin as the twin of Piety. Later on, in the Latin, the word "philanthropia" came to mean both humanity and justice. When Bruno uses the word "philanthropia" in the *Spaccio,* he notes that he uses it because "humanity" did not include enough. The humanists, then, were not understood as meeting the Brunian standard for justice to men. These humanists, *Christian* humanists, found what they wanted in the term "charity". For Bruno, it was *justice* and not charity that was needed by everyman. So Bruno uses the word "philanthropia" with the meaning justice to men. Francis Bacon adopts the term "philanthropia" rather than the term "humanity" for his goal, calling it "the Greek word." Therefore, I take it that Bacon was using it in the Greek sense which meant justice to men. Thus, when Bacon says "philanthropia is my aim", he is not directly referring to anything more than "justice for men." He leaves piety to the Scriptures and the Bishop.

Bacon experimented with codes and wrote in cypher when neces-sary to protect himself. By referring to "the Greek word," philan-thropia, Bacon was probably referring to the primacy of justice over piety. He could have used "humanity", which had been dilated to include both the holy and the just. But he did not. Only those very literate men of his own ilk would get the message.

For Bacon, the inclination for goodness is deeply implanted in man's nature, whether by good habit or by good disposition. If neither good habits nor good disposition are in a man, he "is no better than a kind of vermin." This sounds like Plato, who said "There is nothing quite so bad as a boy, untamed." Bacon also quotes Machiavelli, who pointed out that the Christian faith had sold men out to tyrants. Bacon recommends that one should not be (and he quotes an Italian proverb) "So good, that he is good for nothing." Love of oneself is the pattern, Bacon says, and love of our neighbor is the portrait we paint from that pattern. "And beware how in making the portraiture thou breakest the pattern." In service to others one should not necessarily drop all and follow, because the good habit is *not* enough. Good disposition is also needed along with the good habits. For Bacon, there is a difference between god-loving polity and human polity, which is civil government. This distinction was strong in Philo. Bacon's blueprint for change will balance these two kinds of polity, but the more primary of the two must be human polity.

The Kingdom of Man demonstrates the *power* of God. Infinite possibilities for improvement of the human condition could be realized, if the Idols are set aside, and the power of God allowed to demonstrate itself *through* man in natural philosophy. Mechanical arts, joined to the rational-reflective arts, would be the *planning, development* and *demonstration* of the rationale of the mechanical arts. Natural philosophy has as its practical arm, the physics. Physics has as its practical arm, the mechanical arts.

Metaphysics, on its practical side, is a methodology in the forming of tables to give order and rule to the formation of middle axioms. The cooperation between the physics and the middle axioms will generate a cooperation of the mechanical arts and methodical collection of experimental results. This cooperation will yield implications for the formation of more refined tables, order, rule and more refined middle axioms. These more abstract axioms will lead to suggesting brand new middle axioms and tables which, in turn, will provide a map to the buried treasure of new particulars, previously not looked for or even suspected by human science as being present.

Methodology in philosophy is polity to Bacon. Polity threads its way through all human activity. A study of polity is paramount to one's ability to become politically effective or methodologically effective in *any* serious human pursuit. Around any pole as enervating center there develops a family of integrated activities which compose the metabolism of that pole and support that pole's inertia. This is a healthy state. The macrocosm-microcosm theme of these

days, along with the theme that there was a co-incidence of contraries, were the metaphysical principles upon which rested most
of the empirical and rational systems of thought. Bacon used both
these doctrines extensively. Policy "è gemino" (Abbott, p. 189)
and the victory was in the balanced act. And the balanced act
was properly political; it was one which supported the co-incident
of contraries.

In Book II of the *Novum Organum,* especially, Bacon emphasizes the need for the social milieu to adapt the methodology of a
rigorous inductive science. In his own political career, Bacon used
these popular metaphysical axioms, tested in experience, to forge
middle axioms as his guide. The form of the monarchy was also
the fixed law of its essential nature, that is, dialectical. Bruno wrote
in the *De Monade* (p. 333) that "without contraries, there would
be no virtue and no nobility, because light always shines from out
of a shadow." Bacon wrote that the form of the monarchy dictated
the "filling of the King's coffers" and "the filling of the poor man's
cup." The monarchy was a natural phenomenon to Bacon, one
which had to be respected and obeyed in order that it might be
commanded. The monarchy was the monarch. The monarchy was
also the people. In each subject was the monarch; in the monarch
was each subject. Insofar as one reflected the other, all would
be well.

Bacon lamented that those who administered the law did not
realize that they were not equipped to *write* the law. He also
lamented that his time had many politicos, but no statesmen to
write the law. He was disgusted that this work was being done "by
monks in cells and gentlemen languishing in castles." Bacon says
that it will take a "whole man" to be a learned governor. Then he
states that he is preparing a book on the science of statesmanship.
One must remain where the action is, if he would write law, Bacon
taught. He felt that much of the law in his day was not appropriate
for the times or the government in which he lived. However, he
stated that he would discuss this no further.

The theme which Bacon emphasizes over and over again is
policy "è gemino." This dual nature of state highlights the most
crucial operation, which is frequently missing in politics. This is
the ability to analyze the condition of the state, sensitive to its

latent configurations, and the ability to hunt down methodologically those laws of nature upon which the well-being of the state depends. This means that the state must be seen through its duality of nature and through the duality of its constituent parts. For Bacon, as for Bruno, the essential characteristics of the whole will remain in its tiniest parts.

Bacon was not satisfied with analyses of the state that were merely descriptive (although he did say that this would be a good place to start). He said that Machiavelli had helped because he wrote about what men *did* rather than about what men "ought" to do. What Bacon wanted was illumination of some laws of nature which were convertible into laws of statehood. Then, statehood could be designed by men, on a bed of scientific rock. "Feigned history" fed a need for heroes (*A.L.*, Bk. II, iv, 2).

As in Philo, one must balance the "ancestral customs" and "the political rights" in the concept of a common nation. This nation would (as in the Philonic tradition) be based upon a common body of law, to which reasonable men could give themselves as willing citizens. The emphasis was shifting *from subject to citizened partic-ipant,* and Bacon tried to guide the drawing up of a national frame for this new breed of subject.

First came national loyalty, which entailed the adoption of the rational ideology of the nation. Second came understanding one's generic and contributory role in the nation. The nation was seen as dependent upon each and every man as a law or a principle (the basic particle) of the monarchy. Therefore, as aggregate, every man was the material cause of the monarch. The will of the aggregate was the principle or law of the monarchy and, therefore, the motive cause of the congregate. The monarch was seen as the principle or law of the congregate and, therefore, the formal cause of the monarchy. The Divine Eye of the congregate was seen as the principle, the monarch, and therefore, was the efficient cause of the aggregate. God depended on the king as law or principle of the Divine Will, because the king was chosen by Divine Will.

This was the dialectic of Bacon's Christian monarchical state, which was explained in this way in his own day. There is little doubt in my mind that Bacon could have explained it without the benefit of the scholastic flavor or the Christian monarchical model of his time. However, he was too cautious to do so, as he himself wrote and practiced. For Bacon felt that one should not startle the culture but, rather, "keep the wheels of his mind concentric with the wheels of Providence."

Bacon's legacy appears also to amount to encyclopedic and editorial preparation of a compendium of what he thought were *the most promising ideas of his day*. These compendia seem to be fragments and parts of many classical and contemporary works that were being circulated among the intellectuals of that time. This is easily discernible by any serious student of the period. Bacon's synthesis represents a lot of work, insight, editing, and courage, and these together paint a picture of what Bacon thought was utilitarian for his times and for posterity. They should be printed as an encyclopedic labor of Bacon's. They are a serious compendium by a seasoned, observant, and astute statesman-editor who knew what he was collecting and why he was collecting it. These works provide serious students with a reflection of Bacon's diagnosis of his times and of his recommendations for the future. Bacon was a man of critical and prolonged political experience, and I believe his encyclopedic synthesis was both timely and fruitful. Indeed Bacon trimmed the works he used to make them appropriate to the times, in the hope that they would circulate freely to stimulate the maturation of what he called "the third great period" in the West.

The Preface to the *Novum Organum,* the Preface and the Plan of the Work in the *Instaurata Magna,* and his *Essays* seem to me to be a different matter completely. They appear to be *peculiarly his own*. In the *Essays* Bacon does use a lot of Scriptural, Roman and contemporary writings, as he illustrates almost every central point he has to make. Yet these crucial points, even though they are buoyed up with references to ancient authorities, seem to be a direct result of his *own* impressive experiences. Bacon uses these authorities to express things he might not have wanted to say publicly; however, the insights which he hammers home seem to be original insights from his own reflections upon his own experience (and Bacon had long, concentrated actual experience). The writings listed above are very valuable and should be taken under careful study; as intimated earlier, they deserve more notice and serious comment than they have received over the years. The tone of each Essay and Preface is sombre, lucid, cold, and penetrating, and yet conveys a respect for human intelligence and an understanding of human frailty that Bacon never lost, through all his long years of gargantuan labor and endurance in the front line of political dueling.

In Bacon's day, the role of an encyclopedist was permeated with danger. Any man who dared to gather "all the knowledge in the world" was treading on very thin ice, insofar as much of it could be straightway adjudged heretical or treasonable. Bacon kept reminding the throne that it was not the quantity of knowledge that was the problem; it was the *quality* of knowledge which was the crucial dimension. Bacon would reassure the monarchy that his collection of knowledge was tied to the welfare of the state and was not just an attempt to glorify himself. Elton's *England* (p. 208) thus describes English books and writings from 1200 to 1640:

> . . . the practice of the time encouraged and applauded wholesale borrowing and verbatim description; to use what earlier writers had written showed commendable humility.

But if one chose to use the new writings, then these early compendia of knowledge had to be secreted and guarded and written in cyphers. Our own experience with encyclopedias—a salesman at the door begging us to take one—hardly enables us to appreciate the tremendous challenge that men like Bacon undertook. Here one must suspend twentieth century attitudes toward the encyclopedia for a time and understand the hazardous role of the encyclopedist in Bacon's day.

Bacon was in no position to praise Cusanus or Bruno or Galileo very much. He could not use their works in his collection, openly. In those days, sources generally could not be given, not because the scholar was a plagiarist or a thief, but because so many works were under suspicion and the writer's association with a man could bring arrest and torture or death as that writer's conscience underwent "examination" by the authorities. Bacon therefore not only collected many works; he then adapted them "to the times".

This theme of the "births of the times" is central in Bacon. Like Socrates, he saw himself as a good midwife. He wanted to deliver only that which would not be destructive or destroyed. The consolation was (as Bacon strongly felt) that the full delivery was inevitable; that is perhaps why he reminds his readers constantly that "Truth is the daughter of Time and not the daughter of authority."

2.

FACTS IN HISTORY VERSUS HISTORICAL FACTS

ARISTOTLE HAD MADE the distinction between "what is known to nature" and "what is known to us." Wolfson talks about "facts in history" and "historical facts." In Spedding (VIII, v), facts must give way to historical continuity if facts clash with historical form. Singer is seriously disturbed by what passes for legal accounts of the past and questions the basic integrity of history as a discipline. Emmison (see Bibliography) gives an honest, hard-hitting account of just what archives are all about. There are also theorists who cast a mould (idealism, empiricism, etc.) to hold past events. They see nothing amiss in forcing the events of the past into their mould. Those that do not fit get trimmed off or "interpreted." Falls tells us that the historians simply synthesize dates for the 1582-1752 period. They use the old month and day and the historical-time year. What results is a completely non-existent date such as March 24, 1603, which is supposed to be the date for Elizabeth I's death. Reportedly, she died in England on March 24, 1602, English time.

The problem of how March 26th (the day the year changed in English time for 1582-1752) would be approached, is open to question. If one approaches March from the February *before* it, he does one thing to the date. If one approaches March 26th from the April *after* it, he does another thing to the date.

If an historian decides that the year was 1602, English time, when Elizabeth died, then, to update the year, he changes the date *before* that March on January 1, 1602, and makes it January 1, 1603. Then, when March 24 comes along, it is March 24, 1603. However, he has *updated* by one year all the events of January,

February, and March 1 to 26 of 1602 and put them *one* year ahead of their actual factual international and domestic context, especially since another event, which actually occurred in February, 1602, may be left alone and *not* updated. Then, we have Elizabeth's demise and this non-updated February, 1602, as being over *one year* apart when, in reality, these events were only separated by one *month*.

A conflict of two to three years plagues the history texts of this 1582-1752 period. Historians write narrative and use dates that are not explained. There is no way for any reader to know whether the dates used are written in historical time or domestic English time. Cheney (pp. ix-x) warned about this laxity:

> Throughout this work the terms Old Style and New Style are used with the primary meanings attached to them by the *Oxford English Dictionary;* that is to say, by Old Style we mean the Julian calendar and by New Style the Gregorian, irrespective of the date adopted for the beginning of the year where these systems are in use. The practice of historians, both in England and on the Continent, has varied in the past, and the result is confusion. To use "New Style", as is often done, to denote simply the historical year, which begins on 1 January, is, strictly speaking, incorrect and to be avoided. If the reader will consider the variations in the practice of England, Scotland, and France between the years 1600 and 1752, he will realize at once the danger of laxity in this mattter.

Let us consider an example of how dates become garbled and distorted by translation into theoretical historical time. Suppose that there is an event A that occurs in August, 1602. Suppose that there is an event B that occurs in August, 1603, twelve months later than event A. In domestic English time, the February that comes six months after August, 1602, would have been called February, 1602, because in domestic time the year did not change until March 26. Suppose that historian X looks at this month— February, 1602—and that X decides to translate this date into its modern equivalent. So X changes it to February, 1603. He continues to refer to the following August as August, 1603. He sees that event B in August, 1603, occurs twelve months after event A in August, 1602. Now another historian, historian Y, comes along and looks at what historian X calls February, 1603. Let us suppose that historian Y knows that event B occurs six months after February, 1603, and that event A occurs in August, 1602, but he does not know the time interval between event A and event B. If he is not aware that February, 1603, is already translated from domestic to historical time, he may decide to translate it himself, making it February, 1604. He will then put event B six months later, in August, 1604. Hence, historian Y ends up seeing twenty-four months between events A and B, when in fact there are only twelve.

This entire sequence is typical of the way in which years and intervals have been disordered and disarranged. In this case the interval of time passed was doubled. It may also be noted that a six-month interval between dates can be erroneously compounded by a factor of three. If event B takes place on September 1, 1599, domestic English time, then this event B is six months after event A that takes place on March 1, 1598, domestic English time. But if these dates are taken as historical, rather than as domestic, then the event B is understood to take place eighteen months after event A. In general, if one starts with a much shorter interval, the proportions of the errors are radically increased. Thus if the dates March 20, 1601 and March 30, 1602 are both domestic dates, they are ten days apart. But if they are taken to be in historical time, then they are 375 days apart.

This problem was not so bad in early times, when some annotation was still used. Cyril Falls (p. 12) describes the way dates were translated:

> The dates are given in old style, but taking the year as beginning on 1 January. The Spaniards, of course, used the new style of the Gregorian calendar introduced in 1582. There is, however, a slight complication in Irish correspondence as regards this matter. The old style was official and used normally by Irish and English alike. The mayor of a town employed it as a matter of course. On the other hand, the Irish chiefs in revolt adopted the new style on what are now called ideological grounds, because it was the work of the Papacy. When they wrote to Spain, in which case the scribes were nearly always priests, they used new style. On occasions when dates in or appended to letters in new style are quoted, they are given as they appear, with the letters "n.s." in brackets beside them.

But the problem is especially bad now, if one would depend upon consistent reports about the syntheticizing of dates. The fall of

1599, for example, is a nightmare. The time from Essex's return from Ireland until his execution can be anywhere from five months to sixteen months. This makes a critical difference if one is studying the relation of this execution to other international and domestic affairs. The official record office has arbitrarily *put dates on letters* written back in the 1500's. Someone comes along and disagrees and erases it. The correspondence which survives has been doctored up beyond recognition of time and place. This is too bad, because the intent of these letters cannot be accurately elicited, since the timing is impossible to ascertain. For instance, the letter that Bacon wrote to Essex upon Essex's release from house arrest (because of the Ireland episode) is dated in most of the later literature as July, 1600. Spedding (*Life and Letters*, III, 190) explains that actually the letter that is written *in Bacon's hand* is *undated*. A copy of this letter of Bacon's was made. Either at that time or later, it was dated "July, 1600". This dated copy of the undated original (in Bacon's hand) has been used as the official letter by historians.

The whole problem of what actually occurred in the last ten years of Elizabeth's reign may not matter to anyone but myself. But it does matter to me as a serious scholar on Bacon, Bruno and the transition period in Italy and England. The complete lack of any information *at all* on the life and death of Anthony Bacon, who played such a critical role in Elizabeth I's espionage, is simply inexcusable. Scholars have searched for a record of the funeral, but there is none. Anthony Bacon was an important person in Elizabeth's England, especially from 1592 to the end of the reign. (He lived with Essex and controlled a network of Elizabethan security agents, at home and abroad.) The evidence used to establish the date of his demise, which is usually given as May, 1601, is so tenuous that it is not acceptable. It is supposedly a letter which is anonymous and addressed to Anthony Bacon describing the times. It is supposedly dated May, 1601, and the official statement is that Anthony never got it "because he was already dead." Williams says that Anthony Bacon did not stand trial.

Actually, much of this confusion may not have been necessary. Records may not have been cross checked from one nation to another nation with a mutual aim of frank reconstruction of facts in history. What had been done was that a text had been decided upon:

> I referred earlier in this lecture to the late sixteenth century as in some ways the period of maximum satisfaction bfore the reforms of the last century. I had in mind the blending of the two principles in local government. But central control then came from the monarchy, and now it is from Parliament. Or rather, for I know that you will hasten to correct me, it is from bureaucrats in Whitehall. Maybe you think that the wheel has come full circle back to the sixteenth century, only today it is a Leviathan with which you have to contend. I offer no comment, remembering Raleigh's words, "Whosoever in writing a modern history shall follow Truth too near the heels, it may haply strike out his teeth." I have made my perambulation and am back in the Elizabethan period; and so, like the medieval scribe, I end with
>
> Laus Deo
>
> (Neale, *Essays in Elizabethan History,* p. 224)

Then, after the text has been decided upon, information is gleaned in order to support this text. All nations have an official "text", and each nation's scholars develop a universe of discourse within the confines of an acceptable world history. Men have been discharged from the Calendar office and the archive offices for allowing their releases or editing to depart from the acceptable historical text of the national authorities, historical and political. When historians become enmeshed in perpetuating national texts, they may no longer be scholars at all: they may become political scribes. See Bacon on this (*A.L.,* Bk. II, ii, 12).

Elton (pp. 21-22) gives us this report:

> This means that for the thirteenth, fourteenth and sixteenth centuries we possess a reasonable account of events which can be reconstructed from the words of contemporary writers. The fifteenth is in a much less happy condition: no writer of significance recorded its annals, and what is there is heavily parochial and extremely patchy. Yet, the history of that century has long been fixed in as firm a mould as that given to the thirteenth by Matthew Paris or to the reign of Elizabeth by William Camden. The trouble is that in this case the mould was shaped later: the standard account of the fifteenth century, with its dynastic strife and War of the Roses (a term invented by Sir Walter Scott) was put together in the sixteenth, partly by Vergil and partly by Hall, both of them concerned to play up the Tudor dynasty under which they lived . . . . Unfortunately,

the lead in this has been taken by amateurs as heavily committed to the other side. It should be stressed that the narrative material does not permit much scope or depth to reconsideration, and those who have tried to rewrite fifteenth century history from narratives alone have been heating the air.

Most of the historical writings are of little value for objective scholarship regarding the facts in history. They are only historical facts, which perpetuate a national bias at the expense of scientific method.

Institutions of higher learning have let the students down. Professors do not order books which depart from the "orthodox" views. Libraries do not buy books which depart from the "orthodox" views. Students are simply programmed with the personal and irrational biases of those who write their historical facts to describe what they think should have happened. All through the literature the irrational treatment of figures in history proceeds on the basis of political favorites (the War of the Roses) or religious conviction of the writers. It is unbelievably emotional. I suspect that we need to start all over again with courageous and stout minds and give a candid account of facts in history and throw away our so-called historical facts. If we rationalize away the most trying and poignant days of human conflict, we cannot learn a thing from the past facts which have been wished away. We need *facts in history,* recorded with no over-protective frosting or irrational, feverish drive to "destroy" certain countries and certain figures in history. History should not be a political hindsight. History should be written in a non-judgmental way offering facts with critical opinion but no homicidal dogma.

Much of the literature from English sources includes an apology or a denial for its Italian-Jewish foundations. This is unfortunate. A lot of the literature on Queen Elizabeth I and Francis Bacon, done by the most revered professional historians, is hardly worth reading. But one must read it, if the research is to be objective. One part of this literature ferociously condemns Elizabeth I and Francis Bacon. It is vicious and completely irrational. On the other hand, there is the equally irrational literature which insists that Elizabeth I was without fault and that Bacon is practically a saint.

I would plead for the honest account. Figures in history were merely men and women just like us. Some were more effective in helping human welfare than others. This can only be decided when we have agreed on what constitutes human welfare. And this is where the rub comes in. However, it is possible to lay our definition of human welfare down before our reader and *demonstrate from our commitment on human well-being* what we think this historical figure accomplished. But we must state our biases loud and clear, for they determine how and why one selects, interprets, and alters the facts to suit his own hypothesis. Historians need not persist in the fantasy that they are specially exonerated from laying bare their basic assumptions. They are not. History has not as yet become a descriptive method and therefore their analyses are put to work upon an implicit and rationalized material which makes empirical verifications of their findings impossible. Mark Twain concluded, "all the ink with which history is written is so much fluid bias."

This is no longer excusable. Researchers have a right to expect the ancillary literature to provide a reasonably objective set of facts which could illuminate the common ground where disciplines overlap. Historians have not worried about providing material which can reflect with candor the problems they have with facts in history. This can only be accomplished by a *full demonstration* of their theoretic model, which must accompany all their presentations of fact.

From careful and persistent study and re-study of the last ten years of Bacon's function in Elizabethan England, the following hypotheses-in-history emerge as faintly visible. (More research must be done to either discredit them or establish them.) The deaths of Essex and Bruno may have occurred only one week apart and may have been causally related. The death of the Queen may have occurred two months later, after the purge (Essex, Anthony Bacon, Bruno, etc.). The Queen may have lived another year at the most, disabled, while Robert Cecil bargained with James of Scotland and others. Bacon may have known what really was happening, and may have played an important role in the whole matter. Bacon's rise to power in the nation only begins here with James I. Why? Was his brother Anthony a suicide, or was he executed? This would make a difference in Francis Bacon's later fate. Is there a connection between Galileo's, Vanini's, and Bacon's downfall? Were Galileo's manuscripts found in Bacon's possession by the authorities? Did Tobie and Bellarmine intercede to get Bacon out of the Tower? The answers to many of these questions are important. Was there a purge of free-thinkers in England for some years before the revolution? Bacon praises some aspects of his contemporary Roman Catholic clergy and their contributions to learning in his *Advancement*. Did this, and his friendship with Tobie and his possession of avant-garde natural science manuscripts, get him into trouble? He wrote in Latin and told James in the *Instaurata Magna* that he had purged his works so that they could be read by all religious faiths. These are honest questions and there should be some means of reaching satisfactory accounts about them.

The bribe charge against Bacon is not tenable. Important posts at court were bought and sold as a matter of fact in those times. The machinery of the court was oiled by considerations from suitors in most cases.

There has been a review of the literature on Bacon. This literature has improved a good deal in the current works by men such as Anderson, Farrington, Paolo Rossi, White, and Rabb. These critical, scientific scholars seem to present a respectable study of Bacon as opposed to the mountain of irrational older literature which occurs in this subject. The scope of this book does not allow an analysis of these works. Rather, the purpose of the present study of Bacon has been to set before the reader a new analysis of Bacon's work, as contained in the *Novum Organum* and the *Advancement of Learning* and the *Essays*. The Prefaces of the *Novum Organum* and of the *Great Instauration* are also included here, as well as the *De Augmentis Scientiarum*.

It should be mentioned that Farrington correctly states that Bacon was the father of industrial science and was influenced by Bruno. However, it should be noticed that, under my analysis, the industrial science in Bacon was only the practical correlate to the planned society that would evolve from an empirically based science of polity or statecraft.

Anderson attempts to demonstrate from the works of Bacon that Bacon was an empiricist, but this is again only part of the story. In his second book on Bacon, however, especially in the last chapter on Bacon's precursors, Anderson points to the full-fledged dependence of Bacon's focus upon the works of his precursors.

White makes the distinction in Bacon between provisional and definitive government. I do not find that in Bacon. The practical or the "most useful" was the recommended version for Bacon, and he did not enjoy the scholastic duality which White sees there. Bacon saw, as did Bruno, the poignant difference between human potential and human achievement, but he was a hard and sombre thinker who could endure the facts without putting any logical frosting over them. Bacon writes that one should stand upon the ancient ways with all of one's senses poised toward the future. In this way, Bacon felt that we would not emerge as hasty empirics who would jump ahead ten paces and fall back twenty paces. Bacon would agree rather with Bruno, who says that we may have to back up a number of paces in order to muster the momentum to jump a wide breach. I do not think this is the same as the provisional and definitive distinction that White sees here.

Rabb is correct in seeing Bacon as a social reformer. However, the long roots of Bacon's social reform, which dig deeply into the latent laws of nature, should be brought out. Bacon saw the evolution of the planned human collective as being inexorably tied to the harnessing of all natural resources, human and non-human.

Rossi sees Bacon as the father of technology and as influenced by the technical and empirical movements of his day. But again the challenge which Bacon heralded, as far as I can make out, was the same one Bruno dealt with. It was the pluralism of both induction and deduction. With Bacon, however, this pluralism had to suffer the stringent limitation of a prescribed, regulated design that was worked out ahead of time and tied to utility.

Wolfson (II, 441) discussed Hegel's metaphysical re-statement of the Christian theological conception of history:

> There is much to be said on this conception of the history of philosophy, both for it and against it. One could go on and argue endlessly whether historical facts, and facts in the history of philosophy in particular, are to be studied—to use the language of Aristotle —as known to us or as known by nature, and consequently one could also go on and argue endlessly whether in our attempt to break

up the continuity of historical events into periods, we should look at all for any differentiating characteristics other than those which are visibly known to us and which have palpably proved themselves of consequence in the experience of a great part of mankind who share common beliefs and a common way of life.

3.

"CONGENIAL" RESEARCH AND "CONGENIAL" TEACHING

THE ONE OLDER TREATMENT of Bacon that I wish to discuss is that of Kuno Fischer, whose work on Bacon is very valuable, although I do not agree with all of it. Fischer explains that "We cannot give a synthetical representation of an analytical thinker without perverting his close and logical sequence of ideas into one that is arbitrary and disconnected."

For Fischer, Bacon was out to solve problems. Bacon cites a goal, and reflects about the correct and legitimate means of going after that goal. Fischer points out that for Bacon the goal is always in view. The ends may despotically demand the appropriate means, but these means can produce many ends. Therefore, the method of descending to only one particular is a sad way of using inference for Bacon. Fischer sees exactly Bacon's point. Bacon's insistence that the first thought be the goal, and that the first premise be framed from that consideration, is very well explained in Fischer. Fischer rightly points out that in Bacon, problems were seen as needing solutions, while axioms call for deductions. It is one thing to ask what will follow from an axiom, and quite another thing to ask, "How shall I solve this problem?". Fischer goes so far as to suggest that "A mind whose first thought is not a principle but a problem to be solved and which begins by proposing to itself a goal that is to be reached, is a mind which thinks analytically." Fischer sees Bacon as of this breed, and I agree with him.

Fischer rightly adds: "In some passages the natural philosophy of the Italians shines with its poetic twilight into that of Bacon, and an accurate account of the relation of Bacon to his Italian predecessors would amply repay a special investigation." And again

Fischer maintains: "We content ourselves with the cursory remark that a congenial description of the transition period between the scholastic age and modern times is yet a *desideratum*. What has hitherto been written on this subject scarcely reaches the surface of the matter."

All one need to do is to pick up the Italian works of Bruno written in London between 1583 and 1585 and test Fischer's statement. One will find Bacon throughout these writings, long before Bacon wrote on these matters. In the Latin works of Bruno one finds so much similarity that it would take a complete book to present the demonstration. Bacon was an encyclopedist. What is important is the use Bacon put good ideas to. He was indeed *a shrewd merchant of ideas,* and wasted only what would not fit into the political scene of his times. Bacon's synthesis was his own, and it was designed to solve the problem Bacon posed to himself: How do we inaugurate the Kingdom of Man? In the *Advancement of Learning,* Bacon states that he was working on a book on the science of statecraft. His complaint was that this science was being handled by a miscellany of efforts. For Bacon, the science of statecraft had an integrity of its own and should be accomplished by those who would know what they were talking about. Politics that was approached from the practical goal of mere survival was hardly worth the human effort. Politics that was based upon control and conversion of natural resources would be the worthy pursuit of human effort. From the marriage of politics and empirical natural science would be born the enduring indestructible offspring, existential empire.

We do not have this book of Bacon's. He alludes to the missing part of the *Novum Organum* that was supposed to come before the Interpretation of Nature. He tells us that the subject which is missing can be found in the back of the *Advancement of Learning.* There, in the end of the *Advancement of Learning* we find the work on the Civil state. However, every time he gets into the actual science of the statesman, which would be a planned politic, he says that he must not mix topics about action with topics about learning, and he drops the subject. But it is not long before he finds another occasion to mention again the need for this science and makes reference to the terrible lack of a scientific politic in his times. Then he reminds us again that he should take his own advice and be silent on these matters. I do not know if Bacon ever wrote the work on statecraft. However, his insistence that this work should be the work of a "whole man" and not the work of a monk in a cell or a languishing noble in some castle, makes me think that he felt that he, Bacon, was the man to do it.

Traditionally Bacon's legacy has been seen as that of one of the "British Empiricists: Bacon, Hobbes and Locke". His Idols are taught. It is constantly repeated that "he put weights on the understanding" and that he wrote that "final causes are barren virgins." These philosophical homilies were supposed to establish Bacon as the "father of modern philosophy". Here and there today one reads that Bacon was also a social reformer. He is also seen as the founder of industrial science. And of course there is the school which hails him as a sinister figure who promised a method which he never delivered and as the man who took a bribe.

None of these positions deals with the job that needs to be done. That is, they do not demonstrate from Bacon's own publishings that the legacy of Bacon has never been understood. They do not demonstrate that the above positions are not the result of serious study of Bacon *as he functioned and as he published*. Even when they accurately report what Bacon published, they do not integrate it into the whole of the Baconian project and keep it in perspective. There is no insight into the role of the encyclopedist in the days of Bacon. It is not brought out that a man who gathered all the knowledge in the world, from alchemy to speculative thought systems, was leading a very dangerous and precarious existence.

Men who insist that they are only going to deal with the internal history of science are indeed hard-pressed to explain to us how the internal history can be taken apart from the external vehicles which carried the internal dialogue. *My point is that written science and philosophy is external the minute it is written down.* It is a document and a physical object that belongs to the external reality. These manuscripts and documents are hidden, stolen, passed around. They are copied and modified. They are changed to suit the times or the bias at hand. In short, their history is external. Whether or not they appear to have been printed or signed by this one or that one is sheer accident. These days of the fifteenth and sixteenth centuries when the literature in the natural sciences was written down provided the times with a *huge amount of external paper* which was the focus of government and church scrutiny and study. This study led to the suppression and destruction of some and the rewriting of a great deal of it. In fact, as in the case of Bacon, who had seen what happened in a few short years to Bruno, Galileo, and Vanini, and who helped examine Peacham, the actual manuscript was written in a closed and enigmatic manner in order that it not be burned at once. Those who attempt to deal with the history of ideas by holding that the record can be studied apart from the physical books in which these ideas are made existential objects, are simply not interested in matters "as known to nature". They are only interested in "matters as known to us". They carve out a theoretical chronology based upon historical time (which is completely non-professional from 1582 to 1752). Then they force old documents into their chart according to their preconceived bias as to who must have done what because of national or ethnic superiority. The core data which have been established for centuries must also be protected. As Quine points out, we tend to save the core or inner axioms of our theories and try to modify the outer aspects of the fabric of our theories.

The history of science and philosophy must be completely re-written because the patching needed is too extensive. It must be re-written from the bottom up. This time the purist or the internal historian must face the fact that his data are not disembodied entities that can be observed in the act of theoretical copulation. Rather, his data are social objects, such as books and manuscripts, which are valued and treated according to the social habits of the times in which they are born.

Bacon repeats and repeats this. No one listened to him. Bacon paid dearly for his attempt to summarize the best of the material of his times. And yet, I see no justification for insulting him (who put a lot of material in Latin because he said it was to be in the tongue of posterity) with this kind of statement (Case[1], p. xix):

> But, after all, what books, if not Bacon's *Essays* and Bacon's *Advancement of Learning,* are to be placed first among specimens of English prose, for combined matter and style, for the truest thoughts expressed in the grandest language, for the light of science regulated by the law of eloquence?

[1]Francis Bacon, *The Advancement of Learning and New Atlantis.* World Classics no. 93. Preface by Thomas Case. London: Oxford Press, 1960.

Especially after having written (Case, p. viii):

> After many years, therefore, of preparation, at length, in 1605 (aet. 45), in the prime of his life, and in the first sunshine of the patronage of King James I, Bacon published the *Advancement of Learning*. It is indeed a work which is not merely the expression of a mature mind, but also a kind of summing-up of the Revival of Learning in the sixteenth century.

Case is typical of a whole group of eulogistic writers on Bacon who hold that the "truest thoughts expressed in the grandest language" were exemplified in Baconian publishings. There is absolutely no report about this "Revival of Learning" as being written in Latin and Greek and Hebrew and Arabic and Italian long years before Bacon put it into the budding English prose. These "truest thoughts" are simply passed over in the first passage quoted, as if they originated with Bacon. And the fact that, at the time of Bacon, Elizabeth had hired John Florio to put together the first English dictionary would seriously question the inference that Bacon had a grand language to work with.

Lewis Einstein deals with the problem of *The Italian Renaissance in England*, which led to the campaign *to english* all the materials available in order that the emerging empire of the seventeenth century have a pure national identity. This is when Bacon was chosen as the *father of modern thought*. That is not fair to Bacon. It is no longer necessary, in terms of needs. I suggest that the whole warp in the history of philosophy be ironed out with honesty and good will.

Kuno Fischer made this appeal in the late nineteenth century. His appeal was ignored. He wrote (pp. 274-275):

> This direction was that of the Italian philosophy of nature, which had revived hylozoism,—the living view of nature taken by the Greeks. In the idea of an eternal living matter, the Italian philosophers, as Bacon thought, came into contact with the Greeks—Telesius with Parmenides and Democritus. Here also Bacon himself was in contact with the physical spirit of his immediate predecessors. Everywhere open to the future, his philosophy was not entirely closed against the past. In some passages the natural philosophy of the Italians shines with its poetical twilight into that of Bacon; AND AN ACCURATE KNOWLEDGE OF THE RELATION OF BACON TO HIS ITALIAN PREDECESSORS WOULD AMPLY REPAY

154   *Francis Bacon and Socialized Science*

A SPECIAL INVESTIGATION.¹ But for this purpose the point of view must be taken *within*² the sphere of the Italian natural philosophy, upon which we cannot enlarge here. We content ourselves with the cursory remark that a CONGENIAL DESCRIPTION OF THE TRANSITION PERIOD between the scholastic age and modern times is yet a *desideratum*². What has hitherto been written on the subject scarcely reaches the surface of the matter.

Fischer wrote this *in 1857*. Although, as the mathematics of relativity was ushered into physics, some philosophers tried to repair the history of philosophy, they did not succeed. MacIntyre, Adamson, and others simply were not used in academia. Kristeller and Anderson, working in Bacon and the philosophers of nature of those times, until recently kept strictly to the internal treatment of the material. Only in 1962 does Anderson in a chapter called "Bacon's originality" deal at some length with Bacon's lack of originality. Lately, Kristeller mentions in passing that Bruno and Galileo probably met. Cassirer's 1927 work, *The Individual and the Cosmos in Renaissance Philosophy*, is only today being read a little and used as a text.

Farrington has at last stated in a re-issue of his book on Bacon and industrial science that "If Bacon had any predecessor it was Bruno." The *De Monade* and the *De Immenso* are only two of the Latin works which I have translated out of the Latin with the help of two Latin masters and a classical scholar (our team will shortly have these ready for publication). Here, the concept of man as the co-operator with nature is the theme. Here also, the re-formed intellectual operation for science is explained. These works were published much earlier than Bacon's encyclopedic works. However, although Bacon could not mention Bruno's name, he gathered the work and tried to pass it on.

Cusanus' work is unknown by most students in philosophy, as they are instructed in the "modern emergence of scientific philosophy with Francis Bacon." And yet no actual grasp of the age of transformation is really possible without the study of Cusanus' logic of contraries tied to a negative theology and a positivistic epistemology. Bacon's concern for the "latent process and latent configuration" to be discerned through *comparative enumeration*

¹My accent in capitals
²Fischer's italics

of physical experiments and physical experience using re-formed or direct observation, is simply not understood. The result is that Bacon is accused of talking a lot about a method which he never delivered. This is too bad. Or else, it is held that Bacon originated a new method, and this is even worse.

It is only in the twentieth century that we look longingly back at the more libertine thinkers of the sixteenth century who ushered in the physics of relativity. For we are faced with their insight, as Bruno stated it, that "Nature is not degrees of reality, there are only human degrees of knowing the one reality." The twentieth century man has painfully come to understand that the vast unknown preceded him and expands stubbornly before him as Newton had warned. Men come and men go, but the cosmos, like the Mona Lisa, sits in amused repose with the solitude of her own reasonings. Leonardo's insight remains intact. Today's scientist understands that in his finest hour he captures but the free creations of his own mind. In that mind, there is possible an infinite number of infinite worlds to delight and tantalize him. In the final analysis, human reason succumbs to whole nature and whole nature does not succumb to human reason.

APPENDICES

Appendix A

COPERNICUS AND BACON'S SOCIALIZED SCIENCE

We refer you further to the following excerpts:

1. Preface to *Novum Organum* (1620)

2. *Novum Organum,* Book I: xlv, lx, lxii, lxv, lxxx, lxxxviii, lxxxix, cix, cxvi, cxix, cxxiv.

3. *Novum Organum,* Book II: v, xviii, xix, xx, xxiii, xxiv, xxv, xxvi, xxvii, xxviii, xxxi, xxxiii, xxxiv, xxxv, xxxvi, xxxix, xl, xlv, xlvi, xlvii, xlviii, L.

4. *Aphorisms on the Composition of the Primary History*: ii, iv, vi, vii, viii, ix, x.

5. *Advancement of Learning*: To the King; Book II: ii, 13; viii, 2, 3, 5; ix, 1; xi, 1, 2, 4, 9; xvii, 11; xx, 1, 7, 8; xxiii, 13, 40, 47; xxv, 17.

6. *Essays*: 1, 3, 12, 15, 16, 17, 19, 24, 38, 39, 50, 51, 54, 57, 58.

THE TOBIE MATTHEW LETTER

Most honourable Lord:

It may please your Lordship, there was with me this day one Mr. Richard White, who hath spent some little time at Florence, and is now gone into England. He tells me, that Galileo had answered your discourse concerning the flux and reflux of the sea, and was sending it unto me; but that Mr. White hindered him, because his answer was grounded upon a false supposition, namely, that there was in the ocean a full sea but once in twenty-four hours. But now I will call upon Galileo again. This Mr. White is a discreet and understanding gentleman, though he seem a little soft, if not slow; and he hath in his hands all the works, as I take it, of Galileo, some printed, and some unprinted. He hath his discourse of the flux and reflux of the sea, which was never printed; as also a discourse of the mixture of metals. Those which are printed in his hand are these: the *Nuncius sidereus*; the *Macchie solari,* and a third *Delle Cose, che stanno su l'acqua,* by occasion of a disputation that was amongst learned men in Florence about that which Archimedes wrote *de insidentibus humido.*

I have conceived that your Lordship would not be sorry to see these discourses of that man, and therefore I have thought it belonging to my service to your Lordship to give him a letter of this date, though it will not be there as soon as this . . . I most humbly do your Lordship reverence.

Your Lordship's most obliged servant,

Tobie Matthew.

Brussels, from my
bed, the 4th of
April, 1619

Note that this was the year Vanini was executed. Was this the reason that Mr. White was carrying all of Galileo's work into England?

A.M.P.

BIBLIOGRAPHY

ABBOTT, EDWIN A.: *Francis Bacon.* London: Macmillan Co., 1885.

ADAMS, H. P.: *Karl Marx in His Earlier Writings.* New York: Russell and Russell, Inc., 1965.

AIKEN, LUCY: *Memoirs of the Court of King James the First.* London: Longman *et al.*, 1822. 2 vols.

—————: *Memoirs of the Court of Queen Elizabeth.* London: Longman *et al.*, 1818. 2 vols.

AMOS, ANDREW: *The Great Oyer of Poisoning: The Trial of the Earl of Somerset for the Poisoning of Sir Thomas Overbury in the Tower of London.* London: Richard Bentley, 1846.

An Exact Abridgement of the Records in the Tower of London, from the Reign of King Edward the Second, unto King Richard the Third. Collected by Sir Robert Cotton, revised, rectified, and supplemented by William Prynne. London: William Leake, 1657.

ANDERSON, FULTON H.: *Francis Bacon: His Career and His Thought.* Los Angeles: University of Southern California Press, 1962.

—————: *The Philosophy of Francis Bacon.* Chicago: University of Chicago, 1948.

ATANASIJEVIC, KSENIJA: *The Metaphysical and Geometrical Doctrine of Bruno as Given in His Work De Triplici Minimo.* Translated by George Vid Tomashevich. St. Louis: Warren H. Green, Inc., 1972.

BACON, FRANCIS: *The Advancement of Learning and New Atlantis.* World Classics no. 93. Preface by Thomas Case. London: Oxford Press, 1960.

—————: *The Works of Francis Bacon.* Collected and edited by James Spedding, Robert Leslie Ellis, and Douglas Denon Heath. London: Longman *et al.*, 1858-1874. 14 vols.

BAER, RICHARD A., JR.: *Philo's Use of the Categories Male and Female.* Leiden: E. J. Brill, 1970.

BAGWELL, RICHARD: *Ireland under the Tudors.* London: The Holland Press, 1963. Vol. III.

BAKELESS, JOHN: *Christopher Marlowe.* London: Jonathan Cape, Ltd., 1938.

161

BARFIELD, OWEN: *Saving the Appearances: A Study in Idolatry*. London: Faber and Faber, Ltd., 1957.

BEESLY, EDWARD SPENCER: *Queen Elizabeth*. London: Macmillan and Co., 1892.

BELLOC, HILAIRE: *Wolsey*. Philadelphia & London: J. B. Lippincott Company, 1930.

BENTWICH, NORMAN: *Philo-Judaeus of Alexandria*. Philadelphia: The Jewish Publication Society of America, 1910.

BIRCH, THOMAS: *Memoirs of the Reign of Queen Elizabeth from the Year 1581 till Her Death*. London: A. Millar, 1754. Reprinted New York: AMS Press, Inc., 1970. 2 vols.

BONANSEA, BERNARDINO M.: *The Theory of Knowledge of Tommaso Campanella: Exposition and Critique*. Washington, D. C.: The Catholic University of America Press, 1954.

——————————: *Tommaso Campanella: Renaissance Pioneer of Modern Thought*. Washington, D. C.: The Catholic University of America Press, 1969.

BOWEN, CATHERINE DRINKER: *Francis Bacon, The Temper of a Man*. Boston: Little, Brown and Co., 1963.

BRADFORD, ERNLE: *Drake*. London: Hodder and Stoughton, 1967.

BRODRICK, JAMES: *The Life and Work of Blessed Robert Francis Cardinal Bellarmine, S.J., 1542-1621*. New York: P. J. Kennedy and Sons, 1928. 2 vols.

BRUNO, GIORDANO: *The Candle Bearer (Il Candelaio)*. English version by J. R. Hale. In *The Genius of the Italian Theater*. Ed. Eric Bentley. New York: Mentor, 1964. Pp. 194-314.

——————————: *La Cena de le Ceneri*. A cura di Giovanni Aquilecchia. Torino: Giulio Einaudi Editore, 1955.

——————————: *La Cena de le Ceneri (Le banquet des cendres)*. Translated by Émile Namer. Paris: Gauthier-Villars Éditeur, 1965.

——————————: *La Cena de le Ceneri. Texte Italien* (partial). Edited by Émile Namer. Paris: Gauthier-Villars Éditeur, 1965.

——————————: *De la Causa, Principio e Uno*. Introduzione e commento di Augusto Guzzo. Firenze: G. C. Sansoni, Editore, 1955.

——————————: *De la Causa, Principio e Uno*. A cura di Giuseppe La Rosa. Siracusa: Editrice Ciranna, 1954.

——————————: *De la Causa, Principio e Uno e Scritti Scelti*. A cura di Antonio Renda. Padova: CEDAM Casa Editrice Dott. Antonio Milani, 1941.

——————————: *Des Fureurs Héroïques*. Texte établi et traduit par Paul-Henri Michel. Paris: Société D'Édition "Les Belles Lettres," 1954.

——————————: *Dialoghi Italiani: Dialoghi Metafisici e Dialoghi Morali.* Nuovamente ristampati con note da Giovanni Gentile. Terza edizione a cura di Giovanni Aquilecchia. Firenze: Sansoni, 1957.

——————————: *The Expulsion of the Triumphant Beast.* Translated and edited by Arthur D. Imerti, with an introduction and notes. New Brunswick, N. J.: Rutgers University Press, 1964.

——————————: *La Filosofia Morale.* Ed. Enrico de Falco. Siracusa-Milano: Editrice Ciranna, 1956.

Giordano Bruno's The Heroic Frenzies. A translation with introduction and notes by Paul Eugene Memmo, Jr. Chapel Hill: University of North Carolina Press, 1964.

Jordani Bruni Nolani Opera Latine Conscripta. Faksimile-neudruck der Ausgabe von Fiorentino, Tocco und anderen Neapel und Florenz 1879-1891. Drei Bande in Acht Teilen. Stuttgart-Bad Cannstatt: Friedrich Frommann Verlag Gunther Holzboog, 1962.

BURKE, BERNARD: *Vicissitudes of Families.* London: Longman, Green, Longman, and Roberts, 1863.

The Cambridge History of Later Greek and Early Medieval Philosophy. Edited by A. H. Armstrong. Cambridge: Cambridge University Press, 1967.

CAMDEN, WILLIAM: *Remains Concerning Britain.* London: John Russell Smith, 1870.

CARAMAN, PHILIP: *Henry Garnet 1555-1601 and the Gunpowder Plot.* London: Longmans, Green and Co., Ltd., 1964.

CASPARI, FRITZ: *Humanism and the Social Order in Tudor England.* New York: Teachers College Press, Columbia University, 1954.

CASSIRER, ERNST: *The Individual and the Cosmos in Renaissance Philosophy.* Translated by Mario Domandi. Philadelphia: University of Pennsylvania Press, 1963. German edition 1927.

CHEYNEY, EDWARD P.: *A History of England: From the Defeat of the Armada to the Death of Elizabeth with an Account of English Institutions during the Later Sixteenth and Early Seventeenth Centuries.* New York & London: Longmans, Green and Co., 1914. Vol. I.

Complaint and Reform in England, 1436-1714. Arranged with introductions by William Huse Dunham, Jr. and Stanley Pargellis. New York: Oxford University Press, 1938.

Correspondence of Robert Dudley, Earl of Leycester. Edited by John Bruce. London: John Bowyer Nichols and Son, 1844.

CORYN, M.: *The Black Prince 1330-1376.* London: Arthur Barker, Ltd., 1934.

COUNTER, K. N. S.: *The Framework and Functions of English Law:*

An Introduction to the English Legal System. Oxford: Pergamon Press, Ltd., 1968.

CREIGHTON, MANDELL: *Historical Essays and Reviews*. Edited by Louise Creighton. London: Longmans, Green and Co., 1902.

CROSS, CLAIRE: *The Royal Supremacy in the Elizabethan Church*. London: George Allen, Unwin, Ltd.; and New York: Barnes and Noble, Inc., 1969.

DIETZ, FREDERICK C.: *A Political and Social History of England*. New York: The Macmillan Company, 1927.

DI NAPOLI, GIOVANNI: *Tommaso Campanella: Filosofo Della Restauranzione Cattolica*. Padova: CEDAM Casa Editrice Dott. Antonio Milani, 1947.

DIXON, WILLIAM HEPWORTH: *Personal History of Lord Bacon*. Boston: Ticknor and Fields, 1861.

DODD, ALFRED: *The Martyrdom of Francis Bacon*. London: Rider and Co., 1945.

DRUMMOND, JAMES: *Philo Judaeus*. London: Williams and Norgate, 1888. Vol. I.

DU BOULAY, F. R. H., and BARRON, CAROLINE M., editors: *The Reign of Richard II: Essays in Honour of May McKisack*. London: The Athlone Press, University of London, 1971.

DUNLOP, IAN: *Palaces and Progresses of Elizabeth I*. London: Jonathan Cape, 1962.

EINSTEIN, LEWIS: *The Italian Renaissance in England*. New York: Columbia University Press, 1902.

EISELY, LOREN: *Francis Bacon and the Modern Dilemma*. Lincoln: University of Nebraska Press, 1962.

ELTON, G. R.: *England, 1200-1640*. Ithaca & London: Cornell University Press, 1969.

EMMISON, F. G.: *Elizabethan Life: Disorder. Mainly from Essex Sessions and Assize Records*. Chelmsford: Essex County Council, 1970.

FALLS, CYRIL: *Elizabeth's Irish Wars*. London: Methuen & Co., Ltd., 1950.

FARRINGTON, BENJAMIN: *Francis Bacon: Philosopher of Industrial Science*. London: Lawrence and Wishart, Ltd., 1951.

———————————: *The Philosophy of Francis Bacon*. Liverpool: Liverpool University Press, 1964.

FINCH, HENRY L.: *The Complete Essays of Francis Bacon*. New York: Washington Square Press, Inc., 1963.

FISCHER, KUNO: *Francis Bacon of Verulam*. Translated by John Oxenford. London: Longman, Brown, Green, Longmans, & Roberts, 1857.

FLETCHER, C. R. L.: *An Introductory History of England from Henry VII to the Restoration.* London: John Murray, 1912. Vol. II.

FRAZER, NORMAN: *English History 1485-1603.* London: A. & C. Black, 1908.

FRENCH, ALLEN: *Charles I and the Puritan Upheaval.* Boston: Houghton Mifflin Co., 1955.

FRENCH, PETER J.: *John Dee: The World of an Elizabethan Magus.* London: Routledge & Kegan Paul, 1972.

FROUDE, JAMES ANTHONY: *English Seamen in the Sixteenth Century.* New York: Charles Scribner's Sons, 1895.

——————————————: *History of England from the Fall of Wolsey to the Defeat of the Spanish Armada.* New York: Charles Scribner and Co., 1865-1870. 12 vols.

GARDINER, SAMUEL RAWSON: *A History of England under the Duke of Buckingham and Charles I, 1624-1628.* London: Longmans, Green and Co., 1875. 2 vols.

GARIN, EUGENIO: *Italian Humanism: Philosophy and Civic Life in the Renaissance.* Translated by Peter Munz. New York: Harper and Row, 1965.

GENTILE, GIOVANNI: *Il Pensiero Italiano del Rinascimento.* Firenze: G. C. Sansoni — Editore, 1955.

GILSON, ÉTIENNE: *The Spirit of Mediaeval Philosophy* (Gifford Lectures 1931-1932). Translated by A. H. C. Downes. New York: Charles Scribner's Sons, 1936.

GOODENOUGH, ERWIN R.: *The Politics of Philo Judaeus: Practice and Theory.* New Haven: Yale University Press, 1938.

GREEN, A. WIGFALL: *Sir Francis Bacon.* New York: Twayne Publishers, Inc., 1966.

GREEN, V. H. H.: *The Late Plantagenets: A Survey of English History between 1307 and 1485.* London: Edward Arnold, Ltd., 1962.

GRIMM, HAROLD J.: *The Reformation Era 1500-1650.* New York: The Macmillan Company, 1954.

GUNNELL, JOHN G.: *Political Philosophy and Time.* Middletown, Connecticut: Wesleyan University Press, 1968.

Handbook of Dates for Students of English History. Edited by C. R. Cheney. London: Offices of the Royal Historical Society, 1945.

HARRIS, VICTOR: *All Coherence Gone.* Chicago: University of Chicago Press, 1949.

HARRISON, G. B., editor: *The Letters of Queen Elizabeth.* London: Cassell and Company, Ltd., 1935.

HARVEY, JOHN: *The Plantagenets: 1154-1485.* London: B. T. Batsford, Ltd., 1948.

HAUGAARD, WILLIAM P.: *Elizabeth and the English Reformation: The Struggle for a Stable Settlement of Religion.* London: Cambridge University Press, 1968.

HELMER, OLAF: *Social Technology.* New York: Basic Books, Inc., 1966.

HERBERT, WILLIAM: *The History and Antiquities of the Town and Port of Hastings, Sussex.* London: W. G. Moss, Kennington, 1824.

HOTSON, LESLIE: Marlowe among the Churchwardens, *Atlantic Monthly,* Vol. 138 (1926), pp. 37-44.

HUBER, KARL: *Einheit und Vielheit in Denken und Sprache Giordano Brunos.* Switzerland: Verlag Hans Schellenberg Winterthur, 1965.

HUME, MARTIN A. S.: *The Year after the Armada: And Other Historical Studies.* New York: The Macmillan Company, 1896.

_____: *The Great Lord Burghley: A Study in Elizabethan Statecraft.* New York: Longmans, Green and Co., 1898.

HURSTFIELD, JOEL: *Elizabeth I and the Unity of England.* New York: The Macmillan Company, 1960.

INNES, ARTHUR D.: *Leading Figures in English History: Tudor and Stuart Period.* New York: Libraries Press, Inc., 1967.

JACOB, E. F.: *Henry V and the Invasion of France.* New York: The Macmillan Company, 1950.

JENKS, EDWARD: *Edward Plantagenet (Edward I).* London & New York: G. P. Putnam's Sons, 1901.

KLEIN, ARTHUR JAY: *Intolerance in the Reign of Elizabeth, Queen of England.* Boston: Houghton Mifflin Co., 1917.

KNIGHT, WILLIAM: *Francis Bacon.* London: Blackwood, 1889.

KOT, STANISLAS: *Socinianism in Poland: The Social and Political Ideas of the Polish Antitrinitarians in the Sixteenth and Seventeenth Centuries.* Translated from the Polish by Earl Morse Wilbur. Boston: Starr King Press, 1957.

KOYRÉ, ALEXANDRE: *La Philosophie de Jacob Boehme.* New York: Burt Franklin, 1968.

KRISTELLER, PAUL OSKAR: *Eight Philosophers of the Italian Renaissance.* Stanford: Stanford University Press, 1964.

_____: *Renaissance Thought: The Classic, Scholastic, and Humanistic Strains.* New York: Harper & Row, 1961.

_____: *Renaissance Thought II: Papers on Humanism and the Arts.* New York: Harper & Row, 1965.

LAMB, V. B.: *The Betrayal of Richard III.* 3rd ed. London: The Mitre Press, 1968.

LANG, ANDREW: *James VI and the Gowrie Mystery.* London: Longmans, Green and Co., 1902.

LEHMBERG, STANFORD E.: *Sir Walter Mildmay and Tudor Government*. Austin: University of Texas Press, 1964.

LEMMI, CHARLES W.: *The Classic Deities in Francis Bacon*. Baltimore: The Johns Hopkins Press, 1933.

MACDONELL, JOHN: *Historical Trials*. Edited by R. W. Lee. Oxford: Clarendon Press, 1927.

MARSH, HENRY: *British Documents of Liberty: From Earliest Times to Universal Suffrage*. Rutherford: Fairleigh Dickinson University Press, 1971.

MARX, KARL: *Capital: A Critique of Political Economy*. Edited by F. Engels. Chicago: Charles Kerr and Co., 1932. Vol. I.

——————: *Economic and Philosophic Manuscripts of 1844*. Edited by Dirk J. Struik and translated by Martin Milligan. New York: International Publishers, 1964.

MATTER, JOSEPH ALLEN: *My Lords and Lady of Essex: Their State Trials*. Chicago: Henry Regnery Co., 1969.

McFETRIDGE, N. S.: *Calvinism in History*. Philadelphia: Presbyterian Board of Publication, 1882.

MORLEY, JOHN, editor: *English Men of Letters*. New York: AMS Press, 1968. Reprinted from 1889 edition, London.

NEALE, J. E.: *The Elizabethan House of Commons*. London: Jonathan Cape, Ltd., 1949.

——————: *Essays in Elizabethan History*. London: Jonathan Cape, Ltd., 1958.

——————: *Queen Elizabeth I*. London: Jonathan Cape, Ltd., 1934.

NEILL, STEPHEN: *Anglicanism*. London: Penquin Books, Ltd., 1960.

O'FAOLAIN, SEAN: *The Great O'Neill*. New York: Duell, Sloan and Pearce, 1942.

ORNSTEIN, MARTHA: *The Role of Scientific Societies in the Seventeenth Century*. Chicago: University of Chicago Press, 1928.

OWEN, JOHN: *The Five Great Skeptical Dramas of History*. London: Swan Sonnenschein and Co., Ltd., 1896.

PACKER, GEORGE NICHOLS: *Our Calendar*. Wellsboro, Pa.: Fred R. Miller Blank Book Co., 1892.

Papers Relating to the Navy during the Spanish War, 1585-1587. Edited by Julian S. Corbett. Printed for the Navy Records Society, 1898.

PASOLINI, COUNT PIER DESIDERIO: *Catherine Sforza*. Authorized edition, translated and prepared with the assistance of the author by Paul Sylvester. Chicago: Herbert S. Stone and Co., 1898.

PATERSON, ANTOINETTE MANN: *The Infinite Worlds of Giordano Bruno*. Springfield, Illinois: Charles C. Thomas, Publisher, 1970.

PEARSON, A. F. SCOTT: *Thomas Cartwright and Elizabethan Puritanism 1535-1603*. Gloucester, Mass.: Peter Smith, 1966.

PELSENEER, J.: Gilbert, Bacon, Galilee, Kepler, Harvey et Descartes: Leur relations. *Isis*, No. 50, XVII (1932), pp. 171-208.

Philo: Philosophical Writings. Selections edited by Hans Lewy. Oxford: Phaidon Press, Ltd., 1946.

POLLARD, A. F.: *Henry VIII*. London: Longmans, Green and Co., 1919.

———————: *The History of England: From the Accession of Edward VI to the Death of Elizabeth (1547-1603)*. London: Longmans, Green and Co., 1910.

POOLE, REGINALD: *Studies in Chronology and History*. Collected and edited by Austin Lane Poole. Oxford: Clarendon Press, 1934.

Queen Elizabeth and Some Foreigners. Edited by Victor Von Klarwill. London: John Lane the Bodley Head, Ltd., 1928.

RABB, THEODORE K. and SEIGEL, JERROLD E., editors: *Action and Conviction in Early Modern Europe: Essays in Memory of E. H. Harbison*. Princeton: Princeton University Press, 1969.

RAIT, ROBERT S.: *An Outline of the Relations between England and Scotland (500-1707)*. London: Blackie and Son, Ltd., 1901.

READ, CONYERS: *Lord Burghley and Queen Elizabeth*. New York: Alfred A. Knopf, 1960.

———————: *Mr. Secretary Walsingham and the Policy of Queen Elizabeth*. Hamden, Connecticut: Archon Books, 1967.

———————: *The Tudors: Personalities and Practical Politics in Sixteenth Century England*. New York: Henry Holt and Co., Inc., 1936.

REBHOLZ, RONALD A.: *The Life of Fulke Greville, First Lord Brooke*. London: Clarendon Press, Oxford, 1971.

REES, JOAN: *Fulke Greville, Lord Brooke, 1554-1628: A Critical Biography*. London: Routledge & Kegan Paul, 1971.

Renaissance Philosophy. The Italian Philosophers: Selected Readings from Petrarch to Bruno. Edited, translated, and introduced by Arturo B. Fallico and Herman Shapiro. New York and Toronto: Random House, 1967. Vol. I.

Renaissance Philosophy. The Transalpine Thinkers: Selected Readings from Cusanus to Suarez. Edited, translated, and introduced by Herman Shapiro and Arturo B. Fallico. New York: Random House, Inc., 1969. Vol. II.

ROSSI, MARIO M.: *Alle Fonti del Deismo e del Materialismo Moderno*. Firenze: La Nuova Italia, 1942.

ROSSI, PAOLO: *Francis Bacon: From Magic to Science*. Translated by Sacha Rabinovitch. London: Routledge & Kegan Paul, 1968.

————————: *Philosophy, Technology, and the Arts in the Early Modern Era.* Translated by Salvator Attanasio, edited by Benjamin Nelson. New York: Harper & Row, 1970.

ROWSE, A. L.: *An Elizabethan Garland.* London: Macmillan and Co., Ltd., 1953.

————————: *The England of Elizabeth: The Structure of Society.* London: Macmillan and Co., Ltd., 1950.

————————: *The English Past: Evocations of Persons and Places.* New York: The Macmillan Company, 1952.

————————: *The English Spirit: Essays in History and Literature.* New York: The Macmillan Company, 1946.

SALZMAN, L. F.: *Edward I.* London: Constable and Company, Ltd., 1968.

SEELEY, R. B.: *The Greatest of all the Plantagenets: An Historical Sketch.* London: Richard Bentley, Publisher in Ordinary to Her Majesty, 1860.

SIMONS, ERIC N.: *Henry VII The First Tudor King.* London: Frederick Muller, Ltd., 1968.

SINGER, DOROTHEA WALEY: *Giordano Bruno, His Life and Thought.* New York: Henry Schuman, 1950.

SINGER, EDGAR A., JR.: *Modern Thinkers and Present Problems.* New York: Henry Holt and Company, 1923.

SITWELL, EDITH: *The Queens and the Hive.* London: Macmillan and Co., Ltd., 1962.

SMITH, A. G. R.: *The Government of Elizabethan England.* New York: W. W. Norton & Co., Inc., 1967.

Society and History in the Renaissance. A report of a conference held at the Folger Library on April 23 and 24, 1960. The Folger Shakespeare Library, Washington, 1960. Administered by the Trustees of Amherst College.

SPAVENTA, BERTRANDO: *La Filosofia Italiana nelle sue Relazioni con la Filosofia Europea.* A cura di Enrico Vigorita. Napoli: Alberto Morano Editore, 1938.

STEEL, BYRON: *Sir Francis Bacon: The First Modern Mind.* Garden City, N. Y.: Doubleday, Doran & Co., Inc., 1930.

STEWART, CHARLES D.: The Joints of Time, *Atlantic Monthly,* Vol. 137 (1926), pp. 10-22.

STIMSON, DOROTHY: *The Gradual Acceptance of the Copernican Theory of the Universe.* New York, 1917. Reprinted in 1970 by University Microfilms, Ann Arbor, Michigan.

STONES, E. L. G.: *Edward I.* London: Oxford University Press, 1968.

STRACHEY, LYTTON: *Elizabeth and Essex: A Tragic History.* New York: Harcourt, Brace and Co., 1928.

170   *Francis Bacon and Socialized Science*

STURT, MARY: *Francis Bacon.* London: Kegan Paul & Co., 1932.

TANNER, J. R.: *Tudor Constitutional Documents, A.D. 1485-1603 with an Historical Commentary.* London: Cambridge University Press, 1930.

THOMAS, J. H.: *Town Government in the Sixteenth Century.* London: George Allen & Unwin, Ltd., 1933.

TIMPANARO, SEBASTIANO: *Scritti di Storia e Critica della Scienza.* Firenze: Sansoni, 1952.

TOCCO, FELICE: *Le Fonti Piu Recenti della Filosofia del Bruno.* Roma: R. Accademia Dei Lincei, 1892.

TOUT, T. F.: *Edward the First.* London: Macmillan and Co., Ltd., 1932.

TROILO, ERMINO: *Averroismo e Aristotelismo Padovano.* Padova: CEDAM Casa Editrice Dott. Antonio Milani, 1939.

VICKERS, BRIAN: *Francis Bacon and Renaissance Prose.* Cambridge: Cambridge University Press, 1968.

VON RANKE, LEOPOLD: *A History of England: Principally in the Seventeenth Century.* London: Macmillan and Co., 1875. Vol. I.

WALDMAN, MILTON: *Elizabeth and Leicester.* Boston: Houghton Mifflin Co., 1945.

_____: *Elizabeth and Leicester.* London: Collins Clear-Type Press, 1944.

_____: *Queen Elizabeth I.* Hamden, Connecticut: Archon Books, 1966.

_____: *Rod of Iron: The Absolute Rulers of England.* Boston: Houghton Mifflin Co., 1941.

WALLACE, KARL R.: *Francis Bacon on the Nature of Man: The Faculties of Man's Soul.* Urbana, Chicago, London: University of Illinois Press, 1967.

WARBURTON, W.: *Edward III.* London: Longmans, Green and Co., 1902.

WATSON, ROBERT: *The History of the Reign of Philip the Second, King of Spain.* London: W. Strahan *et al.,* 1777. 2 vols.

_____: *The History of the Reign of Philip the Third, King of Spain.* London: G. Robinson *et al.,* 1783.

WHITE, HOWARD B.: *Peace among the Willows: The Political Philosophy of Francis Bacon.* The Hague: Martinus Nijhoff, 1968.

WILLERT, P. F.: *Henry of Navarre and The Huguenots in France.* London & New York: G. P. Putnam's Sons, 1893.

WILLIAMS, CHARLES: *Bacon.* London: Arthur Barker, Ltd., 1933.

WILLIAMS, NEVILLE: *Elizabeth the First, Queen of England.* New York: E. P. Dutton & Co., Inc., 1968.

WILSON, P. W.: *The Romance of the Calendar.* London: George Allen and Unwin, Ltd., 1937.

WOLFSON, HARRY AUSTRYN: *Philo: Foundations of Religious Philossophy in Judaism, Christianity, and Islam.* Cambridge: Harvard University Press, 1947. 2 vols.

NAME INDEX

SUBJECT INDEX

A

Absolute infinite (*see* Infinite, absolute)
Absolute limit (*see* Limit, absolute)
Absolute maximum
  (*see* Maximum, absolute)
Absolute minimum
  (*see* Minimum, absolute)
Absolutes, the
  description of, 114
Achievement, human
  love and, relationship between, 104
  marriage and, relationship between, 103
  methods of, Baconian, 102-103
    (*see also* Boldness)
  time affecting, 102-103
Action, natural
  basis of, 33
Advancement of Learning, vii, 5, 22, 37,
  39, 40, 43, 44, 45, 60, 79, 89, 97, 98,
  120, 125, 135, 143, 146, 150, 152, 153,
  159
  publication, year of, 7
Aesop, 93-94
Alchemy, 61, 83 (*see also* Magic)
Alexander the Great, 35, 75
Ambition
  theory of, Baconian, 92
Andrews, Clergyman, 51
Animos
  definition, discussion of, 22-23
Anticipatio mentis, 33 (*see also*
  Anticipation, corrected)
Anticipation (*see also* Nature and
  Regolato Sentimento)
  acceptance of
    rationale for, 19
  aspects of, acceptable, 30 (*see also*
    Nature, anticipation of)
  basis of, necessary, 19
  description of, 21-23
  interpretation and, comparison
    between strength of, 32
  rejection of
    rationale for, 19-20, 28

superstition and, relationship
  between, 20
suspension of
  importance of, 20
  types, discussion of, 22
Anticipation, animal
  rejection of, 31
Anticipation, corrected
  concept, acceptance of, 31
  definition of, 33
Anticipation, spontaneous
  rejection of
    rationale for, 20
*Aphorisms on the Composition of the
  Primary History*, 159
Archimedes, 160
Aristotle, 35, 100, 118, 139
  criticism of, Baconian, 38, 52
Arts
  ideal, description of, 40
Arts, mechanical
  nature and, relationship between, 14
Assumptions, false
  definition of, 28
  examples of, 28
Astronomy
  mathematics and, relationship
    between, 38
  study of
    criticism of, Baconian, 39-40
Atheism
  discussion of, 123-124
Authority
  elements of, base, 105
  ideal, description of, 105 (*see also*
    Integrity)
  truth and, relationship between, 117,
    138 (*see also* Time)
Axioms (*see also* Fact)
  axiom of, 71-72
  formulation of
    foundation for, 63
    process of, 28
    tables during, use of, 28

177

human, 35
House of Commons (*see* Commons,
House of)
Human Habits (*see* Habits, human)
Humanism
criticism of, Brunian, 132

I

Immortality
attainment, methods of, 76
Induction
definition of, 31
use of, reformed, 34
Infinite
description of, Brunian, 112-113
Infinite, absolute
description of, Brunian, 112-113
Infinite Worlds of Giordano Bruno,
vii, 109
Innovation (*see also* Conformity
and Reformation)
description of, Baconian, 120-121
nature of, contrary, 121
support of, national
difficulties of, 121
Instaurata Magna, 34, 136, 146
Integrity
laws of, latent, 106
learning of, 105
Intellect, human (*see also* Faculties,
human)
development of, balanced, 13
Interpretation
anticipation and, comparison between
strength of, 32
Interpretation, legitimate
limits of, 36
Interpretation of Nature (*see also*
Nature, Interpretation of)

J

James I, 55, 60, 84, 101, 145, 146, 153
Bacon and, relationship between
Francis, 10
court, description of, 85
Parliament and, power struggle
between, 56
reign of
problems of, 84-85
Judgment
discovery of, sequential, 45
passing of
tradition affecting, 45
rules, system of, 45

suspension of, necessary, 13
(*see also* Eucatalepsia)
Justice
administration of
nation and, relationship between
integrity of, 96
administration of, ideal
description of, 125
corruption of
effects of, 96
implementation of
theories of, Baconian, 78

K

Kant, Immanuel, 92
Knowledge
aquisition of (*see also* Learning)
approach to, Baconian, 62-63, 74
insatiability of, 75
discovery of
conditions for, 21
foundations of, 21
maturation of, "causal", 87
maturation of, "effective", 87
power of
factors affecting, 131
power and, comparison between
martial, 63
power and, relationship between
human, 65
theory of, Cusan, 112-114, 129
types of, balance between
reason affecting, 117
Knowledge, civil
goals of, 87-88
Knowledge, human
acquisition of
concern with, political, 72
process of, 28
tradition and, relationship
between, 44
advancement of (*see also* Judgment,
discovery of)
controversy affecting, 44 (*see also*
Bacon, Francis, conformist guise
of) philanthropia and, relationship between, 44-45
goals of, 28 (*see also* Force,
utilitarian)
man and, relationship between
evolution of, 121-122
passing of
tradition affecting, 45
power and, relationship between